SURVIVAL ENGLISH

English Through Conversations

Book 2

SECOND EDITION

Lee Mosteller
San Diego Community College District

Michele Haight
California State University Fresno

Illustrated by Jesse Gonzales

Longman

D0144374

Acquisitions editor: Nancy Leonhardt
Director of Production and Manufacturing: David Riccardi
Editorial production/design manager: Dominick Mosco
Electronic/production supervision, interior design,
    page composition, realia and cover design: Wanda España
Electronic Art: Rolando Corujo and Todd Ware
Cover Design Coordinator: Merle Krumper
Production Coordinator: Ray Keating

Illustrations by: Jesse Gonzalez

20 19 18 17 16

ISBN 0-13-016650-2

Preface

This book is designed for the ESL student who has a limited oral vocabulary, a limited reading ability, and some use of the alphabet. The student is probably not functionally literate or fluent in English. *Survival English: English Through Conversations, Book 1* provides a helpful prerequisite to this book. Students at this level bring to the classroom common experiences from the community and the motivation to learn the survival skills necessary to function in daily life.

This book is organized to develop listening, speaking, reading, and writing skills, in that order. It provides competency-based dialogues in nine content areas appropriate for the low-literature or beginning high adult learner. The dialogues provide listening and speaking practice incorporated with familiar and necessary living skills. They are followed by charts, reading passages, sequence stories, and exercises to reinforce and develop the competencies introduced in the dialogues. The writing activities are patterned to provide the learner with much practice at a low level and based on language patterns the learner can orally produce.

OBJECTIVES

1. To teach the most basic functional language patterns in survival situations.

2. To teach language patterns and vocabulary in a systematic and controlled manner.

3. To develop reading and writing skills based on what the student can produce orally.

4. To provide survival information and coping skills necessary for adult living.

ACKNOWLEDGMENTS

Our special thanks to Gretchen Bitterlin and many other ESL teachers in the San Diego Community College District.

Contents

1

SCHOOL

A. I want to learn

> to speak English.
> to drive.
> to sew.
> to weld.
> to use the computer.
> citizenship.

B. You can go to school.

A. Where?

B. Adult school.

A. When?

B. I'm not sure. Let's look in the schedule.

FALL 1993
Class Schedule

Center Classes
Begin August 23, 1993
End December 20, 1993

Adult School Schedule

CLASS	DAY	TIME	LOCATION	TEACHER
ESL 1,2,3	M, W, F	8:30 - 11:30	High School	May
Driving	F	1:00 - 3:00	Church	North
Computer Intro.	M, W	5:30 - 8:30	High School	Hart
Sewing	Th	6:00 - 9:00	Junior High	Johnson
Citizenship	T	6:00 - 9:00	Junior High	Smith

Answer the questions:

1. What time is the ESL 3 class _____

2. What day is it? _____

3. Where is it? _____

4. Who teaches it?_____

5. What time is the citizenship class? _____

6. Where is it? _____

7. What day is it? _____

8. Who teaches it? _____

9. What time is the computer class? _____

10. Where is it? _____

11. What day is it? _____

12. Who teaches it? _____

> **HOW to REGISTER**
>
> Start by getting an application for registration at the adult center. Our hours are 8 am to 9 pm Monday through Friday. The center is closed on the week-ends. You may also register in the class on your first day.

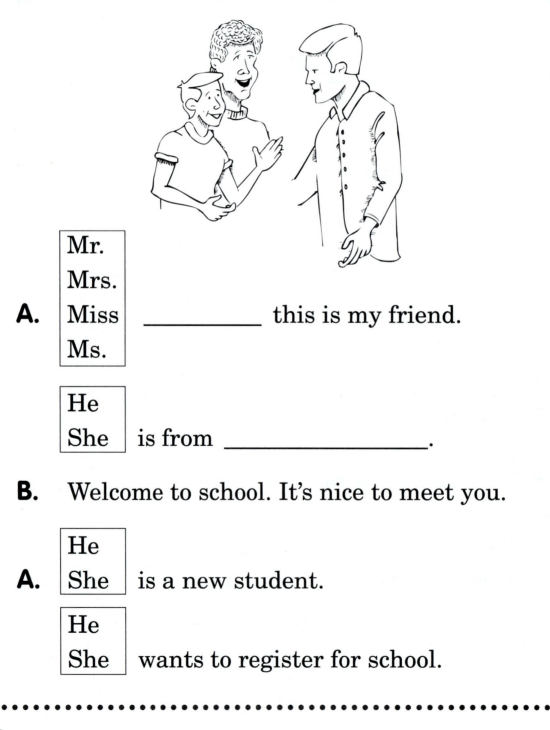

A. | Mr.
Mrs.
Miss
Ms. | _____ this is my friend.

| He
She | is from _____.

B. Welcome to school. It's nice to meet you.

A. | He
She | is a new student.

| He
She | wants to register for school.

A. Welcome to school. Here's your registration card. Please fill it out.

B. I forgot my social security number.

A. That's O.K. Bring it tomorrow.

B. O.K. I will.

• •

Fill in the registration card:

ADULT SCHOOL REGISTRATION CARD

Name _____
              Last   First

Address _____
            Number   Street

_____
       City   State   Zip Code

Telephone _____

Soc. Sec. No. _____

Date of Birth _____

In case of emergency call _____

Phone _____

citizen ☐   immigrant ☐   refugee ☐   unknown ☐

Signature _____

Date _____

Complete the sentences.

1. My name is _____.
2. My address is _____.
3. My telephone number is _____.
4. My social security number is _____.
5. My teacher's name is _____.
6. I'm from _____.
7. I speak _____.

Ask your classmate.

8. My classmate's name is _____

_____.

9. _____ address is _____.
10. _____ telephone number is _____.
11. _____ is from _____.
12. _____ speaks _____.
13. We study _____.
14. We study at _____.

A. Oh no!

B. What's the matter?

A. I can't find my pencil.
I think I forgot it.

B. Here. Borrow mine. I have an extra one.

• •

Complete the sentences.

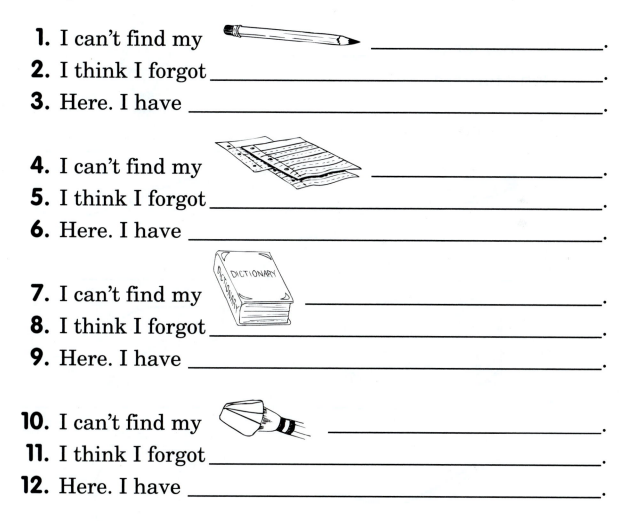

1. I can't find my _____.

2. I think I forgot _____.

3. Here. I have _____.

4. I can't find my _____.

5. I think I forgot _____.

6. Here. I have _____.

7. I can't find my _____.

8. I think I forgot _____.

9. Here. I have _____.

10. I can't find my _____.

11. I think I forgot _____.

12. Here. I have _____.

A. See you tomorrow.

B. O.K.

A. Remember to bring a notebook.

B. I will.

A. Don't forget to bring a pencil.

B. I won't.

· ·

Remember to _____.

Don't forget to _____.

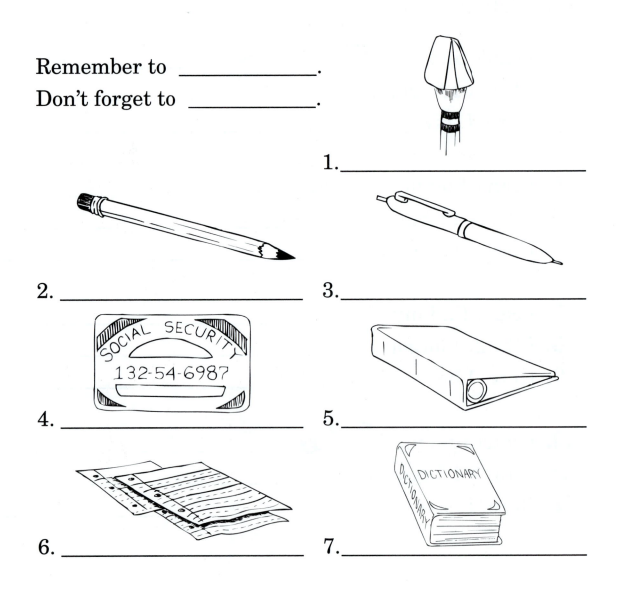

1._____

2._____ 3._____

4._____ 5._____

6._____ 7._____

A. Is anyone sitting here?

B. I'm not sure. Ask him.

A. Is anyone sitting here?

C. No, sit down.

A. Is anyone using this dictionary?

B. No, help yourself.

A. Thank-you.

Read the Chart:

it	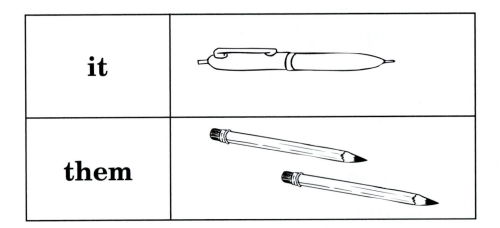
them	

Use the chart to complete the sentences.

1. I can't find my pens.

I forgot_____.

2. He can't find his dictionary.

He forgot_____.

3. They can't find their papers.

They forgot_____.

4. She can't find her social security card.

She forgot_____.

5. We can't find our pencils.

We forgot_____.

6. He can't find his eraser.

He forgot_____.

7. She can't find her registration card.

She forgot_____.

8. They can't find their notebooks.

They forgot_____.

A. Do you have little | children?
                          grandchildren?
                          _____?

B. Yes, I do

A. Who takes care of them?

B. My | husband.
           wife.
           babysitter.
           _____.

A. Do they go to | preschool?
                     nursery school?
                     day care?

B. No, they don't. They're on the waiting list
for preschool.

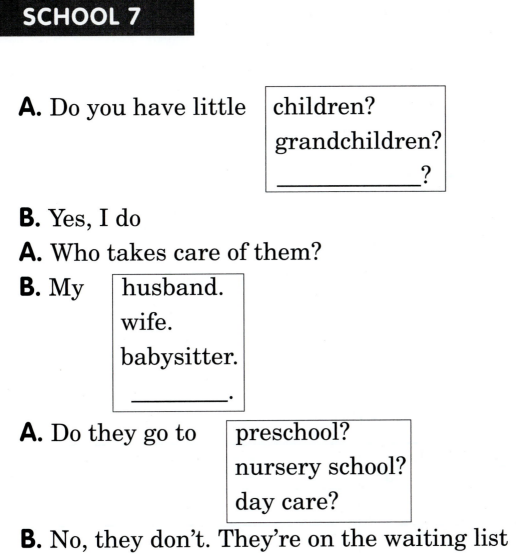

DAY CARE CENTER

A. Are your children in school?

B. Yes, they are.

A. What school do they go to?

B. My son goes to elementary school.

He's in fourth grade.

My daughter goes to high school.

She's in tenth grade.

• •

Write about your children.

Name	Age	School	Grade

Ask about your classmate's children.

Name	Age	School	Grade

AGE	GRADE	SCHOOL
2 3 4		**nursery school or pre-school**
5 6 7 8 9 10 11	**kindergarten** 1 _____ 2 _____ 3 _____ 4 _____ 5 _____ 6 _____	**elementary**
12 13 14	7 _____ 8 _____ 9 _____	**junior high or middle school**
15 16 17	10 _____ 11 _____ 12 _____	**senior high**
18 19 20...		**adult job training vocational college**

Write the word next to the grade.

first   second   third   fourth   fifth   sixth

seventh   eighth   ninth   tenth   eleventh   twelfth

Use the chart on the previous page.
Complete the sentences.

1. La is eight years old.
   He's in _____ grade.
   He goes to _____ school.

2. Xanh is sixteen years old.
   He's in _____ grade.
   He goes to _____ school.

3. Xay is four years old.
   She's in _____ school.

4. Tom is fourteen years old.
   He's in _____ grade.
   He goes to _____ school.

5. Phai is twenty-six years old.
   She goes to _____ school.

6. Anna is five years old.
   She's in _____.
   She goes to _____ school.

7. Joe is fifty-three years old.
   He goes to _____.

8. I'm _____ years old.
   I go to _____.

A. I'm not coming tomorrow. I have to go to my daughter's school.

B. What's the matter?

A. Nothing. She's getting an award.

B. That's great news.

· ·

I'm	not
He She It	isn't
We You They	aren't

I	have to
He She It	has to
We You They	have to

Complete the sentences.

1. I _____ coming. I _____ go to my daughter's school.

2. They _____ coming. They_____ talk to their son's teacher.

3. She _____ coming. She _____ talk to her daughter's teacher.

4. The teacher _____ coming. She_____ go to a meeting.

A. My name is _____ .

My 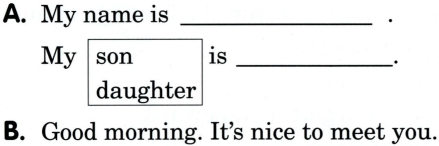 is _____.

B. Good morning. It's nice to meet you.
I want to talk to you about his report card.

A. How is he doing?

B. He's doing very well. He works hard.

• •

GRADES

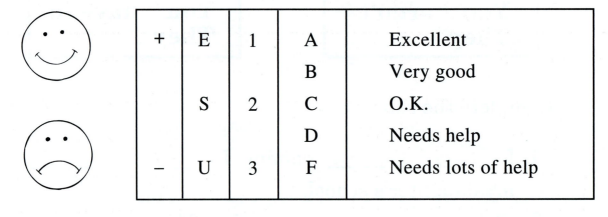

	+	E	1	A	Excellent
				B	Very good
		S	2	C	O.K.
				D	Needs help
	−	U	3	F	Needs lots of help

A. Good morning, Mrs. Johnson.

B. Hello, Mr. North. How is my daughter doing in school?

A. Her behavior is excellent, but her spelling is not very good.

B. Can you give her some extra homework in spelling?

A. Yes, I can. She needs to work more on her spelling.

ELEMENTARY REPORT CARD	
NAME:	GRADE
READING	C
WRITING	C
SPELLING	D
MATH	B
P. E.	B
CITIZENSHIP	A
DAYS ABSENT: 1	DAYS TARDY: 0

Read the report card.

REPORT CARD

STUDENT'S NAME: ANN DIN   GRADE: 7

SUBJECT	FIRST	SECOND	THIRD	FINAL
READING	C	B	A	B
ENGLISH	B	C+	B	B
SPELLING	A	A−	B+	A
MATHEMATICS	A	A	A	A
SCIENCE	C	B	A	B
PHYSICAL EDUCATION	S	S	S	S
MUSIC	S	S	S	S
SOCIAL STUDIES	S	S	S	S
BEHAVIOR	E	E	E	E
DAYS ABSENT	1	0	2	3
DAYS TARDY	0	3	1	4

Match

1. Spelling _____   a. Un_t_d St_t_s
2. Math _____   b. Singing
3. Music _____   c. H_2O
4. Science _____   d. 32+76=?

REPORT CARD				
STUDENT'S NAME: ANN DIN		GRADE: 7		
SUBJECT	FIRST	SECOND	THIRD	FINAL
READING	C	B	A	B
ENGLISH	B	C+	B	B
SPELLING	A	A-	B+	A
MATHEMATICS	A	A	A	A
SCIENCE	C	B	A	B
PHYSICAL EDUCATION	S	S	S	S
MUSIC	S	S	S	S
SOCIAL STUDIES	S	S	S	S
BEHAVIOR	E	E	E	E
DAYS ABSENT	1	0	2	3
DAYS TARDY	0	3	1	4

Use the report card to answer the questions.

1. How many days was Ann late?

_____

2. How many days was Ann absent?

_____

3. What is her final grade in English?

_____

4. What is her final grade in math?

_____

5. Did her science grade go up or down?

_____

6. Did her spelling grade go up or down?

_____

7. What is her final grade in music?

_____

8. What is her final grade in reading?

_____

9. How is her behavior?

_____

A. School Office.

B. This is _____ . My son can't come to school today. He's sick.

A. What's his name?

B. His name is _____ .

A. What grade is he in?

B. He's in the _____ grade.

A. O.K. Thank you for calling. I'll tell his teacher.

• •

| She | She's | her |

1. My daughter can't come to school today. _____ sick.

2. What's _____ name?

3. _____ name is Anna.

4. What grade is _____ in?

5. _____ in second grade.

6. I'll tell _____ teacher.

Letters

When children are absent from school, they usually need a letter to return to school. Every letter has five important parts:

      1. the date

      2. the person's name you are writing to

      3. what you want to say

      4. a good-bye or thank-you

      5. the person's name who wrote the letter

> Feb. 28, 1993
>
> Dear Teacher,
>
>   Tom was sick. Please excuse him from school.
>
>   Thank-you,
>   Mrs. Day

Read the letter and answer the questions.

1. What's the date? _____

2. Who is the letter to? _____

3. What's the matter? _____

4. Is there a good-bye or a thank-you?

_____

5. Who wrote the letter? _____

On Monday, November 19, Tom had a dentist appointment. He was late for school. Help his mother, Mrs. West, write a letter to his school.

Dear _____ _____

_____

_____

_____

_____

_____

_____

_____

Check your work.   Answer the questions.

CIRCLE ONE

1. I wrote the date.   yes   no

2. I wrote someone's name.   yes   no

3. I wrote about something.   yes   no

4. I wrote thanks or good bye.   yes   no

5. I signed my name.   yes   no

Children often bring home letters from school. They are important. Here is a letter about a trip the children will take. Fill in the letter.

April 20

Dear Parents,

The second grade is going on a field trip to the city zoo on Monday, April 28 by bus. Please fill out this form and return it to school.

Thank-you,
Lincoln School

- -

My son/daughter _____
(student's name)

has my permission to go to the _____
(place)

on _____ by bus.
(date)

_____
parent's signature

_____
date

Answer the questions.

1. Who is this letter to?

_____

2. Who is the letter from?

_____

3. What is the letter about?

_____

4. What's the date of the letter?

_____

Tell the story.

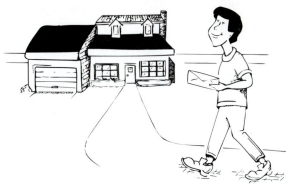

Read the story.

Faissal's Conference

Faissal brought home a letter from school. The letter was from his teacher. His teacher wanted to talk to his parents. He wanted to have a conference. Faissal's parents went to the school. They met the teacher. They shook hands with the teacher. They talked about Faissal. His report card was very good. Faissal and his parents are proud.

Circle true or false.

1. Faissal brought home a letter.   true   false

2. The letter was from the school nurse.   true   false

3. Faissal's parents went to Faissal's school.   true   false

4. Faissal is a terrible student.   true   false

5. Faissal's parents and teacher had a conference.   true   false

Write the true sentences here.

_____

_____

_____

_____

Answer the questions.

1. What did Faissal bring home from school?

_____

2. Who was the letter from?

_____

3. What was the letter about?

_____

4. Where did Faissal's parents go?

_____

5. What did the teacher and Faissal's parents talk about?

_____

6. How was his report card?

_____

7. Why was Faissal happy?

_____

8. Why were Faissal's parents proud of him?

_____

Complete the sentences.

Faissal _____ home a letter from school. The letter
_____ from his teacher. His teacher _____
to talk to his parents. He _____ to have a conference.
Faissal's parents _____ to the school. They
_____ the teacher. They _____ hands
with the teacher. They _____ about Faissal. His
report card _____ very good. Faissal and his parents
_____ proud.

FROM: TEACHER

TO: PARENTS
NOVEMBER 12, 1993

Review the Unit 1 dialogues. Complete the sentences.

1. I want to learn to speak _____.

2. I want to register for _____.

3. I remember my _____ and _____.

4. I go to _____ school.

5. La is eight years old. He goes to _____ school.

6. La is a very good student. He has many A's on his

_____ _____.

7. There are five important parts in a _____.

ELEMENTARY REPORT CARD	
NAME:	GRADE
READING	C
WRITING	C
SPELLING	D
MATH	B
P.E.	B
CITIZENSHIP	A
DAYS ABSENT: 1	DAYS TARDY: 0

FALL 1993
Class Schedule

Center Classes
Begin August 23, 1993
End December 20, 1993

2

CLOTHING

A. _____ had a new baby.
B. Let's buy her a present.
A. That's a good idea.
B. Does she need baby blankets?
A. Yes, I think she does.

· ·

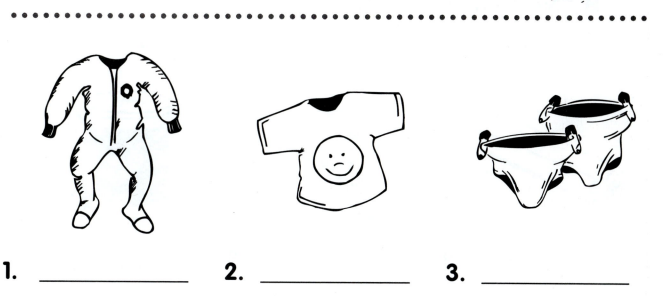

1. _____   2. _____   3. _____

The Len family had a new baby. They need baby clothes.
They need T-shirts and sleepers. They need diapers and
blankets too.

1. Do they have a new baby?_____
2. Do they need baby clothes? _____
3. Do they need diapers?_____
4. Do they need blankets?_____
5. Do they need sleepers? _____

A. How much of this do you need?

B. Three yards.

A. O.K. It's $2.98 a yard. Do you need a zipper or thread?

B. No, thanks. Just the fabric.

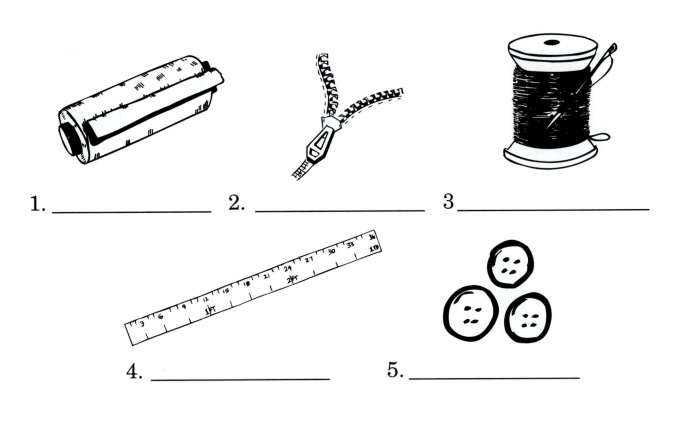

1. _____   2. _____   3 _____

4. _____   5. _____

1 yard is _____ inches.

1/2 yard is _____ inches.

1/4 yard is _____ inches.

1/3 yard is _____ inches.

A. Your jacket is beautiful.

B. I can make you one. What size do you wear?

A. I wear a size 10.

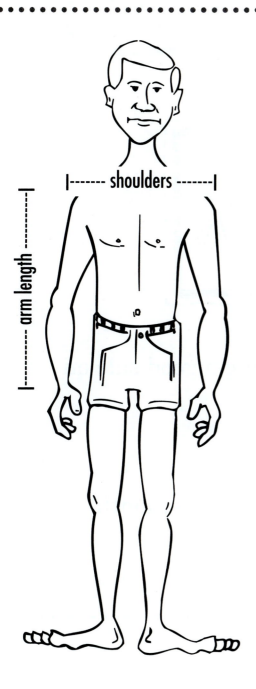

shoulders

arm length

Women, what size do you wear?

I wear size _____ pants.

I wear size _____ dress.

I wear size _____ blouse.

I wear size _____ shoes.

Men, what size do you wear?

I wear size _____ pants.

I wear size _____ shirt.

I wear size _____ shoes.

A. _____ is having a good sale on clothes this week.

B. What's on sale?

A. Sweaters and pajamas for kids.

B. I can't afford to buy anything this month. Maybe next month.

A. Let's go window shopping then.

A. Can I help you?
B. No, thanks. I'm just looking.

A. Can I help you?
B. Yes, please. I'm looking for _____ .

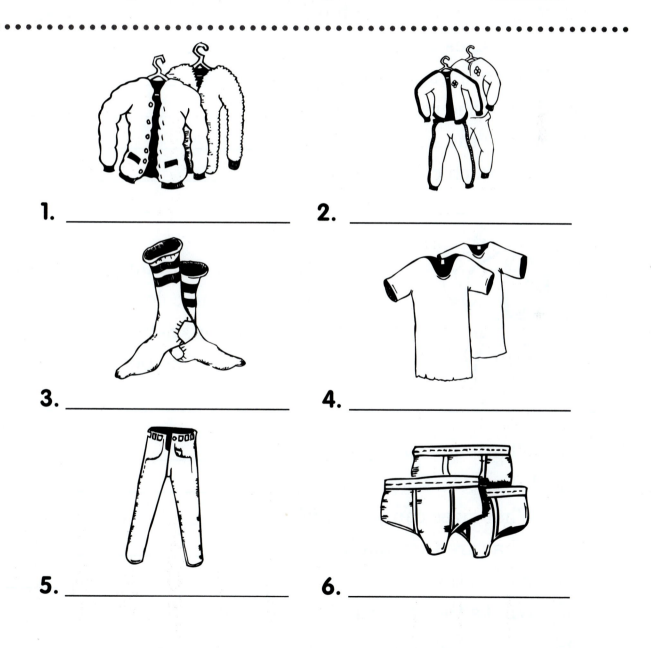

1. _____

2. _____

3. _____

4. _____

5. _____

6. _____

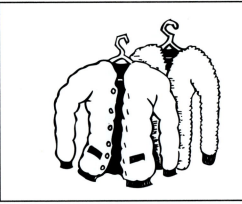

Sweaters $7.99 each, reg. $9.00.
Many colors and styles.
Women's S-M-L.
Cotton-polyester knit.

1. What's on sale? _____

2. What colors can you buy? _____

3. What sizes can you buy? _____

4. What are they made of? _____

5. What's the regular price? _____

6. What's the sale price? _____

7. How much can you save? _____

50% off Men's and Ladies' warm-ups.
Many styles and colors.
Polyester-cotton. S-M-L-XL.
Regular $25.00-$30.00

8. What's on sale? _____

9. What colors can you buy? _____

10. What sizes can you buy? _____

11. What are they made of? _____

12. What's the regular price? _____

13. What's the sale price? _____

14. How much can you save? _____

Read the chart. Can you find the missing prices?

Regular Price	50% off saves you	30% off saves you	20% off saves you
$1.00	.50	.30	.20
$2.00	$1.00	.60	.40
$3.00	$1.50	.90	.60
$4.00	$2.00	$1.20	.80
$5.00		$1.50	$1.00
$10.00	$5.00		$2.00
$15.00	$7.50	$4.50	
$20.00		$6.00	$4.00
$25.00	$12.50		$5.00
$50.00	$25.00	$15.00	
$100.00			

Fill in the chart, and answer the questions.

	Regular	20% off	You Pay
	$15.00		
	$25.00		
	$10.00		
	$20.00		

1. What's the regular price of the pants? _____
2. How much can you save on the pants? _____
3. How much are the pants on sale? _____
4. What's the regular price of the sweaters? _____
5. How much are the sweaters on sale? _____
6. What's the regular price of the sleepers? _____
7. How much are the sleepers on sale? _____
8. How much are the jogging suits on sale? _____

A. How do these pants look?

B. They look a little short.

A. You're right. I think I want a longer pair.

B. Here, try these on.

OPPOSITES

small   _____

short   _____

expensive   _____

long   _____

big   _____

cheap   _____

1. These pants are too small.

I need _____ ones.

2. This dress is too long.

I need a _____ one.

3. This coat is too expensive.

I want a _____ one.

4. These shoes are too big.

You need _____ ones.

5. This shirt is too short.

You need a _____ one.

6. These jeans are too long.

You need _____ ones.

A. How does this shirt look?

B. It looks nice.

A. Is it cheaper than the red shirt?

B. Yes, it is. It's cheaper than the red one.

• •

$25.00 $5.00 $17.50

Is it **cheaper** or more **expensive**?

1. The pants are _____ than the dress.

2. The T-shirt is _____ than the dress.

3. The T-shirt is _____ than the pants.

4. The pants are _____ than the T-shirt.

5. The dress is _____ than the T-shirt.

6. The dress is _____ than the pants.

Store A   Store B   Store C

1. Which store has a sale on Saturday and Sunday?

_____

2. Which store has a three day sale?

_____

3. Which store has a 1/2 off sale?

_____

4. Which stores have sales on everything?

_____

5. Which store has the lowest prices on sale?

_____

6. Which store is the most expensive?

_____

A. Are you next?

B. Yes, I want this blanket.

A. Will this be all?

B. Yes.

A. It's $24 plus tax.

B. Oh. $24?

A. Yes.

B. I'm sorry. I thought it was $14.

A. Do you still want it?

B. No, thanks. That's too much.

A. No problem.

• •

What does the price tag say?

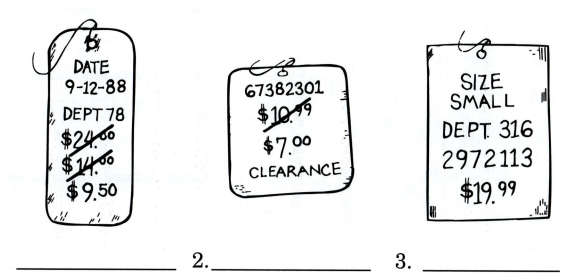

1. _____   2. _____   3. _____

Tell the story.

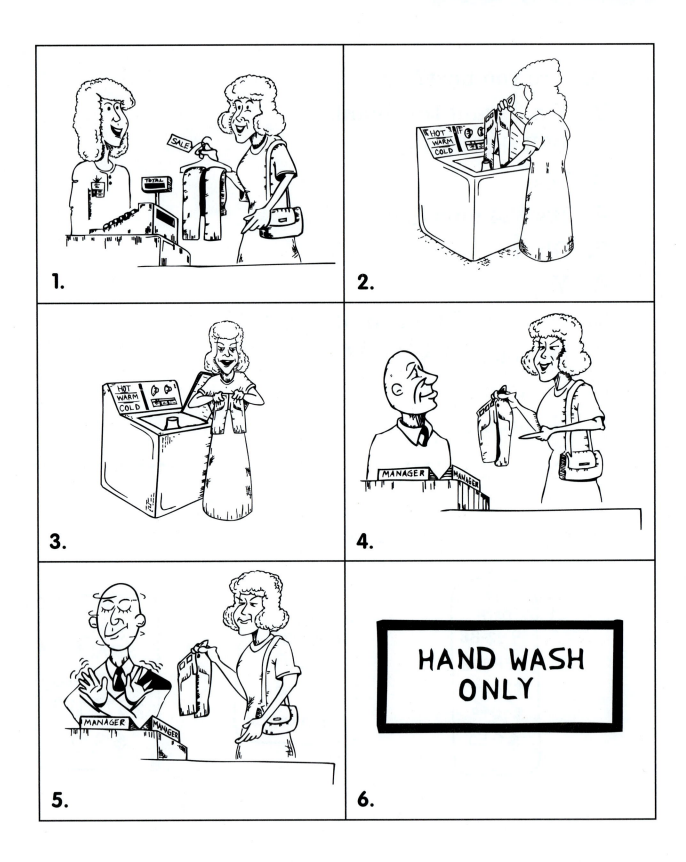

1.

2.

3.

4.

5.

6.

HAND WASH ONLY

Read the Story.

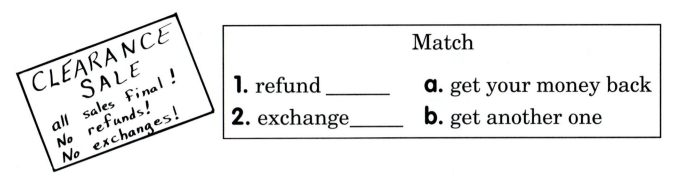

Match

1. refund _____   **a.** get your money back

2. exchange_____   **b.** get another one

Joni and the Jeans

Joni was happy to see the jeans. The jeans were on the clearance table. They were 50% off. She bought them for her son. They were not too big and not too small. They fit her son well. Then Joni washed the jeans. They shrank a lot. Now they were too small for her son. Joni took the jeans back to the store. The store manager didn't take them back because Joni bought them on a clearance sale. Next time Joni will read the label and the sale sign carefully.

Circle true or false.

1.	Joni bought a pair of jeans.	true	false
2.	The jeans were 30% off.	true	false
3.	The new jeans fit her son well.	true	false
4.	Joni washed the jeans and they shrank.	true	false
5.	Joni got her money back.	true	false
6.	It's important to read the labels inside clothes.	true	false
7.	It's important to read the sale signs	true	false

Answer the questions.

1. Who bought the jeans?

   _____

2. Who were the jeans for?

   _____

3. Did Joni buy the jeans on sale?

   _____

4. Did Joni read the label in the jeans?

   _____

5. Why did Joni take the jeans back to the store?

   _____

6. What will Joni do next time she sees a clearance table?

   _____

Use the answers from above to write the story.

                    _____

_____

_____

_____

_____

_____

_____

_____

Clothing Labels

It is important to read the labels in clothes. The labels tell the sizes, and they tell how to wash the clothes. The labels will tell you if you can wash them in the washing machine. All clothes have labels. Read the labels carefully, and write the label under the picture that shows you how to wash it.

1. hand wash
2. preshrunk
3. machine wash
4. do not machine wash
5. cotton-polyester
6. wool
7. permanent press
8. silk
9. 100% cotton

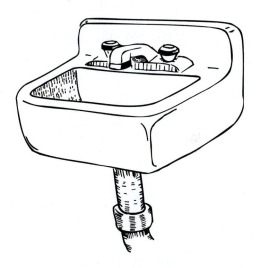

Wash these in the washing machine;

Wash these in the sink;

_____

_____

_____

_____

_____

_____

_____

_____

_____

_____

Read the clothing labels and answer the questions.

A.
100% Wool
Product of USA
Hand wash only
M   10-12

1. What size is it? _____
2. What's it made of? _____
3. Can I put it in the washer? _____

B.
Small
Machine Washable
Cotton-Polyester
Hong Kong

4. What size is it? _____
5. What's it made of? _____
6. Can I put it in the washer? _____

C.
Ladies L
Hecho en Mexico
Do not machine wash
Silk

7. What size is it? _____
8. What's it made of? _____
9. Can I put it in the washer? _____

D.
35% Cotton 65% Polyester
Machine Wash Warm
Made in Taiwan
Preshrunk   XL

10. What size is it? _____
11. What's it made of? _____
12. Can I put it in the washer? _____

E.
100% Cotton
Machine Wash and Dry
6X
Made with price in the USA

13. What size is it? _____
14. What's it made of? _____
15. Can I put it in the washer? _____

A. Where are the sweatshirts?

B. Look upstairs in the sportswear department.

A. Is the shoe department upstairs too?

B. No, it isn't. It's downstairs.

A. Thanks

 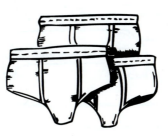 

Match

1. baby clothes _____   **a.** sportswear dept.

2. shoes _____   **b.** baby dept.

3. sweatshirts _____   **c.** shoe dept.

4. towels _____   **d.** jewelry dept.

5. watches _____   **e.** housewares dept.

6. tables _____   **f.** furniture dept.

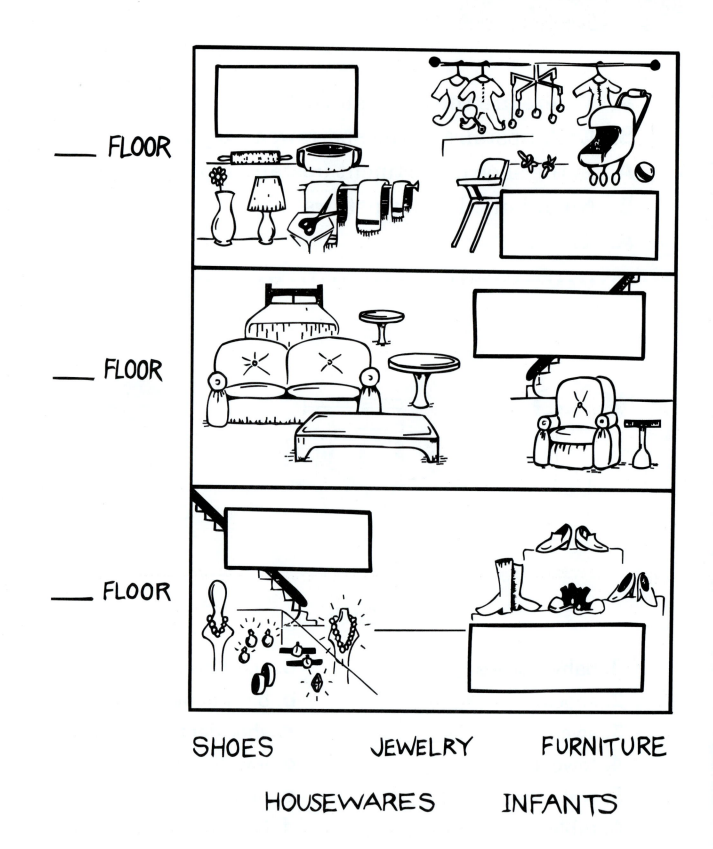

___ FLOOR

___ FLOOR

___ FLOOR

SHOES   JEWELRY   FURNITURE

HOUSEWARES   INFANTS

1. Where are the boots?

They're in the _____ department on

the _____ floor.

2. Where are the watches?

They're in the _____ department on

the _____ floor.

3. Where are the shoes?

They're in the _____

on the _____ .

4. Where are the chairs.

They're in the _____ on the

_____ .

5. Where are the towels?

They're in the _____

on the _____ .

6. Where are the baby sleepers?

They're in the _____

on the _____ .

7. Where are the lamps?

They're in the _____

on the _____ .

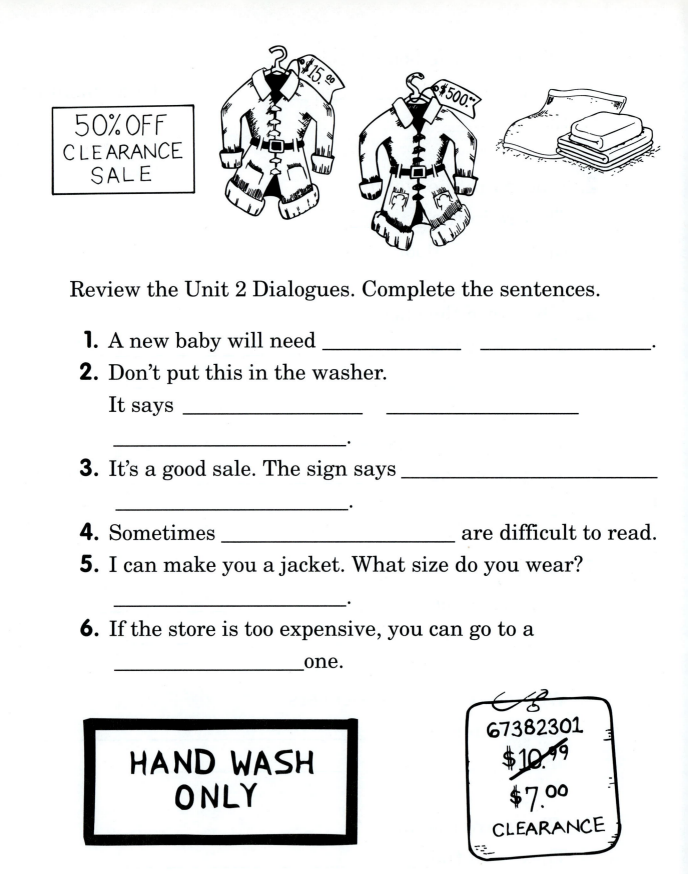

Review the Unit 2 Dialogues. Complete the sentences.

1. A new baby will need _____ _____.

2. Don't put this in the washer.

   It says _____ _____

   _____.

3. It's a good sale. The sign says _____

   _____.

4. Sometimes _____ are difficult to read.

5. I can make you a jacket. What size do you wear?

   _____.

6. If the store is too expensive, you can go to a

   _____one.

3

FOOD

A. What's on sale this week?

B. Look at the ad.

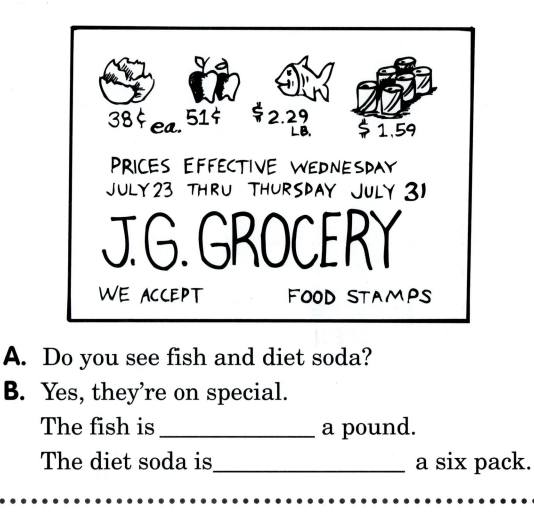

38¢ ea. 51¢ $2.29 LB. $1.59

PRICES EFFECTIVE WEDNESDAY
JULY 23 THRU THURSDAY JULY 31

J. G. GROCERY

WE ACCEPT   FOOD STAMPS

A. Do you see fish and diet soda?

B. Yes, they're on special.

The fish is _____ a pound.

The diet soda is_____ a six pack.

• •

Match

1. ounce _____   **a.** lb.

2. pound_____   **b.** doz.

3. each _____   **c.** fl.

4. dozen _____   **d.** ea.

5. fluid _____   **e.** oz.

The sign says:

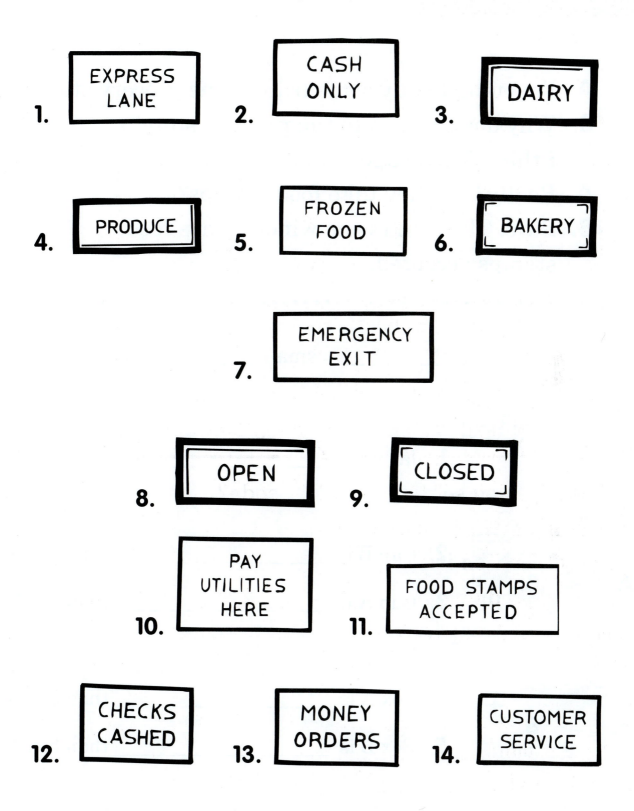

1. EXPRESS LANE

2. CASH ONLY

3. DAIRY

4. PRODUCE

5. FROZEN FOOD

6. BAKERY

7. EMERGENCY EXIT

8. OPEN

9. CLOSED

10. PAY UTILITIES HERE

11. FOOD STAMPS ACCEPTED

12. CHECKS CASHED

13. MONEY ORDERS

14. CUSTOMER SERVICE

a. Where can I pay my electricity bill?
b. Where is the bread?
c. Where is the milk?

A. I'm going to buy some fruit at the grocery store.

B. Why don't you go to the produce store?
I think it's cheaper.

A. Really? Do they take food stamps?

B. Sure. The sign in the window says food
stamps accepted.

• •

cheap _____ big _____ small _____ large _____

A. 50¢ **B.** $1.00   **1.** Jar A is _____than jar B.

A. **B.**

2. Can B is _____then can A.

3. Can A is _____than can B.

A. **B.**

4. Box A is _____than box B.

5. Box B is _____than box A.

A. **B.**

6. Bottle A is _____than bottle B.

7. Bottle B is_____than bottle A.

The Produce Store

Joe is going to the produce store. He's going to buy some bananas and apples. He thinks the produce store is cheaper than the grocery store. He thinks the fruits and vegetables are fresher, too.

1. Is Joe going to the produce store?

_____

2. What is Joe going to buy?_____

_____

3. Why is Joe going to the produce store?_____

_____

4. Do you go to a produce store?

_____

5. Do you think the produce store has fresher fruits and vegetables?

_____

6. Do you think the produce store is cheaper than the grocery store?

_____

A. This line is the shortest. Let's get in it.

B. We can't. The sign says ten items or less.

A. You're right. We have too many things.

· ·

More or Less

1. $10.00 is _____ than $9.00.

2. $1.00 is _____ than $.50.

3. $9.98 is _____ than $9.89.

4. $36.00 is _____ than $37.00.

5. $50.38 is _____ than $53.08.

6. $29.00 is _____ than $28.99.

7. $99.00 is _____ than $100.00.

8. $47.33 is _____ than $46.00.

9. $100.00 is _____ than $50.00.

10. $500.00 is _____ than $5.00.

11. $91.00 is _____ than $19.00.

12. $65.00 is _____ than $6.50.

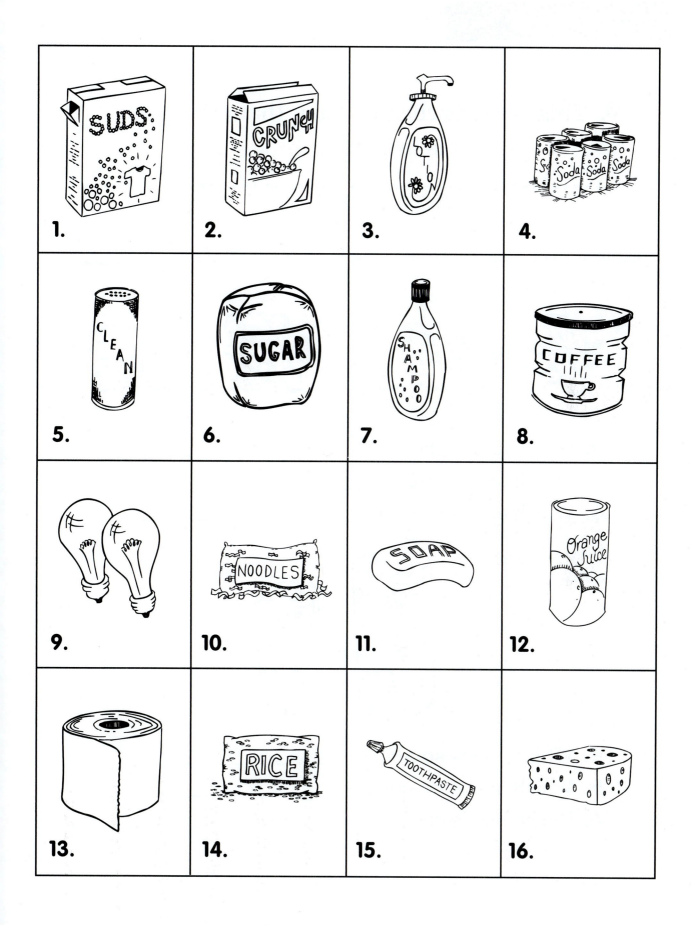

1.

2.

3.

4.

5.

6.

7.

8.

9.

10.

11.

12.

13.

14.

15.

16.

A. This bread is cheaper than that one.

B. But this loaf is larger.

• •

1 pound = 16 ounces   1/2 pound = 8 ounces   1 1/2 lbs. = _____

1. Which one is cheaper? _____

2. Which one is larger? _____

3. Which one is fresher? _____

4. Which one is smaller? _____

5. Which one is fresher? _____

6. Which one is cheaper? _____

A. Excuse me. Where's the shampoo?

B. It's on aisle 12 near the hand lotion.

A. I looked on aisle 12, but I didn't see it.

B. It's on the top shelf near the end.

A. Thanks. I'll look again.

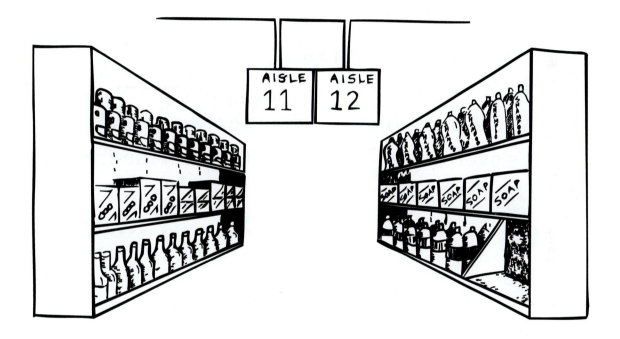

Find the Opposites

1. top_____   **a.** small

2. front _____   **b.** expensive

3. large_____   **c.** bottom

4. cheap _____   **d.** back

A. Is this diet soda on sale?

B. No, it's not.

A. Where can I find the soda that's on sale?

B. It's over there. It's next to the caffeine-free soda.

A. Thanks.

• •

Match

1. caffeine free _____

2. low sodium _____

3. sugar free _____   **a.** no salt

4. diet _____   **b.** no caffeine

5. decaffeinated _____   **c.** no sugar

6. low calorie_____

7. sodium free_____

A. Where's the detergent that's on special?

B. On aisle 2.

A. Are the rebate forms there too?

B. No, they're not. The rebate forms are at the customer service desk.

A. Thanks.

$ 2.00 REBATE

SEND IN THIS FORM WITH THE RECEIPT AND THE UPC SYMBOL FROM KLEEN.

NAME:_____

ADDRESS:_____

_____

J G
GROCERY

DETERGENT. 4.50

ORANGES... 1.00

PAPER........59

COOKIES.....1.29

TOTAL   7.38

CASH.......10.00

CHANGE....2.62

THANK YOU

2. _____

45671

456790

3. _____

1. _____

Where's the _____ that's on special?

Where are the _____ that are on special?

1. _____

   that's on special?

2. _____

   that's on special

3. _____

   that are on special?

4. _____

   that's on special.

5. _____

   _____?

6. _____

   _____?

Complete the sentences.

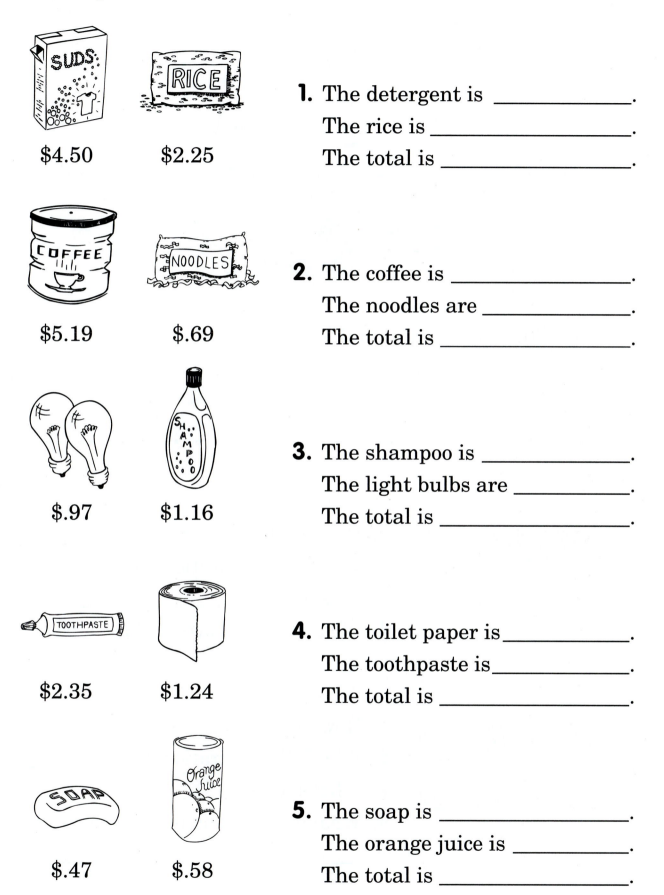

$4.50 $2.25

1. The detergent is _____.
 The rice is _____.
 The total is _____.

$5.19 $.69

2. The coffee is _____.
 The noodles are _____.
 The total is _____.

$.97 $1.16

3. The shampoo is _____.
 The light bulbs are _____.
 The total is _____.

$2.35 $1.24

4. The toilet paper is _____.
 The toothpaste is _____.
 The total is _____.

$.47 $.58

5. The soap is _____.
 The orange juice is _____.
 The total is _____.

A. That comes to $10.97.

B. I have a coupon.

A. O.K. The new total is $10.47.

• •

A.

1. How much do you save? _____
2. What's the expiration date? _____
3. What's it for? _____
4. What store will accept this coupon?

_____

B.

5. How much do you save? _____
6. What's the expiration date? _____
7. What's it for _____
8. What store will accept this coupon?

_____

A. Excuse me. I think there's a mistake here.

B. What's the problem?

A. Does this say $4.19 for bananas?

B. Oh, no. You bought a little more than four pounds. The bananas were $1.05.

A. Thanks for your time.

B. If you have more questions, please ask.

- -

HAPPY MARKET		
4.19 lb bananas	@ 4/100	1.05
2 lb apples	@ 3/100	.67
3.50 lb oranges	@ 2/100	1.75
	Total	3.37
Have a Nice Day		

1. Circle the total.

2. How much are the bananas a pound? _____

3. How much are the apples a pound? _____

4. How much are the oranges a pound? _____

HAPPY SUPERMARKET

8527 Main Street
4-8   9:12 A.M.

4.19 lb	@ 4/100	
bananas		1.05
meat		2.31
meat		2.64
orange juice		.69

Total	6.69
Eligible	6.69
Cash due	.00
Stamp TND.	10.00

.31 change
3.00 food stamp change

You Get a Good Deal

Answer the questions.

1. What's the total? _____

2. What's the total eligible for food stamps? _____

3. How much change in cash is there? _____

4. How much change in food stamps? _____

5. What's the date on the receipt? _____

6. What store is this?_____

A. Let's dye some eggs.
B. What do we need?
A. We need _____.

1.  _____

2.  _____

3. _____

4. _____

5.  _____

Making Easter Eggs.

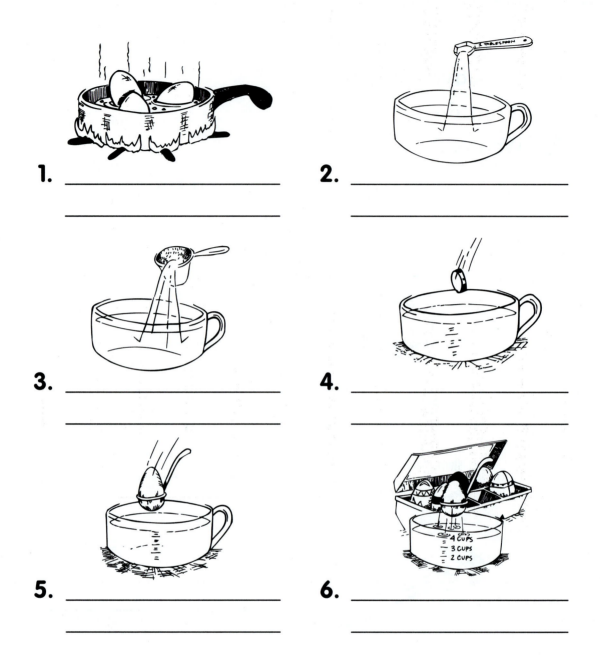

1. _____

2. _____

3. _____

4. _____

5. _____

6. _____

Write the sentences in order under the correct picture.

Put 1 tablespoon vinegar into cup.

Take out eggs and let dry.

First, hold-boil clean white eggs.

Dip eggs into colored water.

Add 1/2 cup cold water.

Drop tablet into vinegar and water.

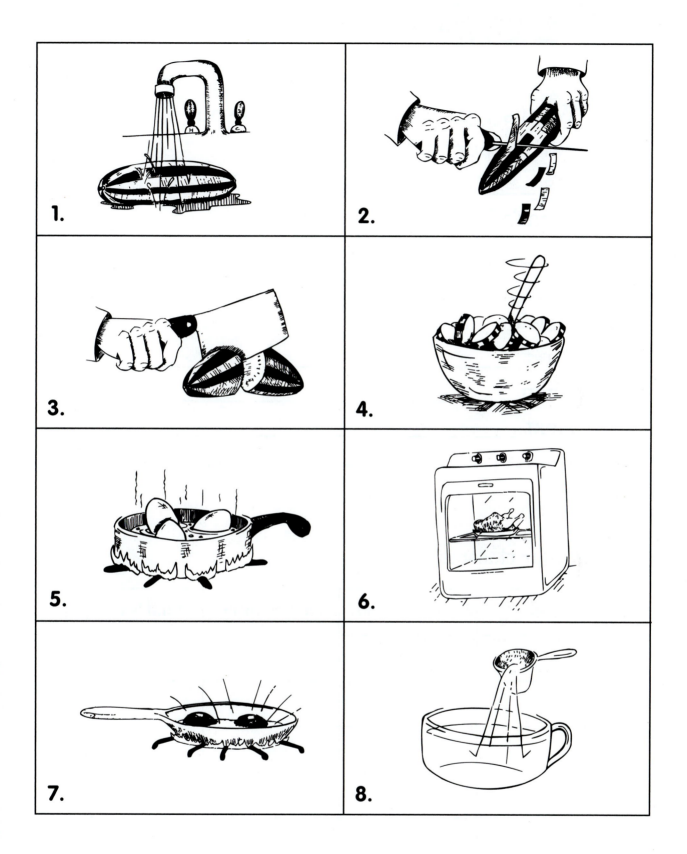

1.

2.

3.

4.

5.

6.

7.

8.

A. What's your favorite food from your native country?

B. It's _____ . I really like it.

A. What's in it?

B. _____

_____ .

A. How do you make it?

B. First _____

Then _____

Next _____

• •

Ask your classmates.

Name	Favorite Food?	What country?	What's in it?
1.			
2.			
3.			
4.			
5.			

A. I bought this milk yesterday, but it's sour.

B. What's the date on the carton?

A. It's January 17.

B. I think you should return it.
Today is only the fourteenth.

· ·

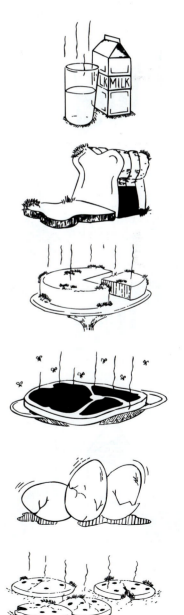

1. This milk is sour.

2. This bread is stale.

3. This cheese is moldy.

4. This meat is spoiled.

5. These eggs are broken.

6. These cookies are stale.

Answer the questions

Today is March 10.

1. What's the date on the carton?

_____

2. Is it fresh? _____

Today is November 22.

3. What's the date on the carton?

_____

4. Is it fresh? _____

Today is September 3.

5. What's the date on the carton?

_____

6. Is it fresh? _____

Today is April 6.

7. Which carton is fresher?

_____

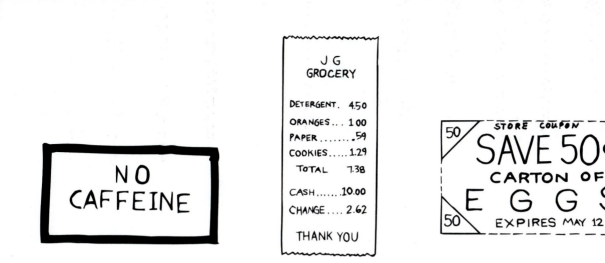

Review the Unit 3 dialogues. Complete the sentences.

1. If you buy _____ _____,

return it.

2. _____ is my favorite food from my

native country.

3. Always remember to check your_____.

4. If you can't have caffeine, look for the words

_____ _____.

5. You can save a little money if you remember to

use a_____.

6. Let's read the _____ to see what's on sale.

4

HEALTH

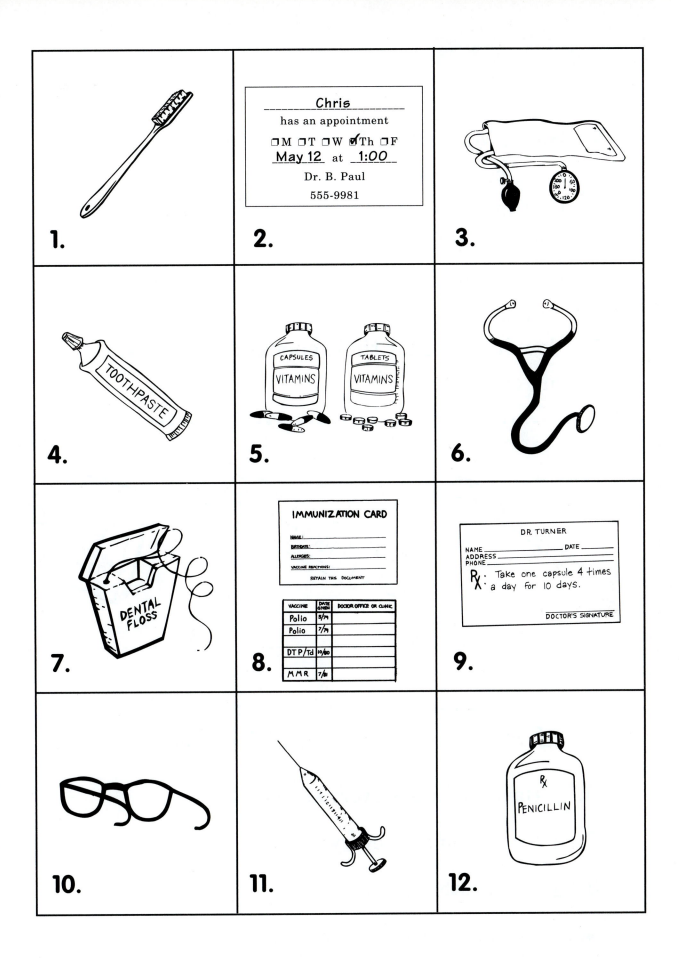

1.

2.
_____Chris_____
has an appointment
☐M ☐T ☐W ☑Th ☐F
__May 12__ at __1:00__
Dr. B. Paul
555-9981

3.

4.

5.
CAPSULES
VITAMINS
TABLETS
VITAMINS

6.

7.
DENTAL
FLOSS

8.
IMMUNIZATION CARD
NAME:
BIRTHDATE:
ALLERGIES:
VACCINE REACTIONS:
RETAIN THIS DOCUMENT

VACCINE	DATE GIVEN	DOCTOR OFFICE OR CLINIC
Polio	5/79	
Polio	7/79	
DT P/Td	10/80	
MMR	7/81	

9.
DR. TURNER
NAME_____ DATE_____
ADDRESS_____
PHONE_____
Rx: Take one capsule 4 times a day for 10 days.
DOCTOR'S SIGNATURE

10.

11.

12.
Rx
PENICILLIN

A. Hello, Mrs. Vang. It's nice to see you again.

B. It's nice to see you too.

A. Do the children brush their teeth after every meal?

B. Well, sometimes they do, and sometimes they don't.

A. Now it's time for their check-ups, x-rays, and cleanings.

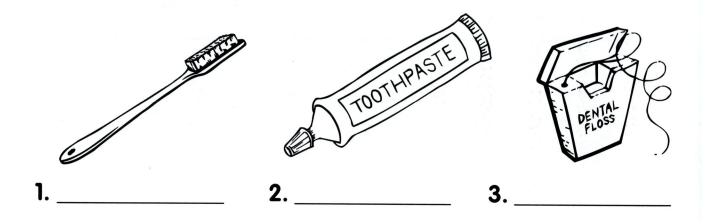

1. _____ 2. _____ 3. _____

Checklist for Dental Health

☑ what is important for good dental health.

1. ❑ Have check-ups every six months.

2. ❑ Brush and floss everyday.

3. ❑ Eat healthy foods.

4. ❑ Eat lots of sweets.

A. Why are you squinting?

B. I can't see very well.

> Everything looks blurry.
> My eyes burn.
> My eyes hurt.
> I get headaches.
> I can't see up-close.
> I can't see far away.

A. You should get your eyes checked. Maybe you need glasses.

B. Where do I go?

A. Make an appointment with an eye doctor.

1. Make an appointment.
2. Have an eye examination.
3. Get a prescription for glasses.

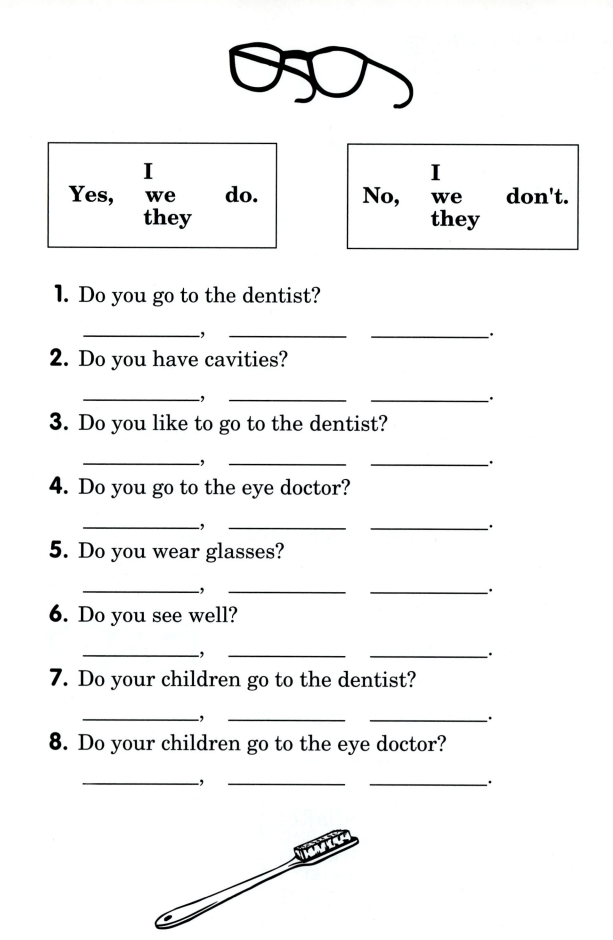

Yes,	I we they	do.

No,	I we they	don't.

1. Do you go to the dentist?

_____, _____ _____.

2. Do you have cavities?

_____, _____ _____.

3. Do you like to go to the dentist?

_____, _____ _____.

4. Do you go to the eye doctor?

_____, _____ _____.

5. Do you wear glasses?

_____, _____ _____.

6. Do you see well?

_____, _____ _____.

7. Do your children go to the dentist?

_____, _____ _____.

8. Do your children go to the eye doctor?

_____, _____ _____.

A. Your son should take vitamins.

B. Vitamins? Are they good for him?

A. Yes, they are. They're important for his health.

· ·

There are many different kinds of vitamins. Ask your doctor which vitamins are the best for you.

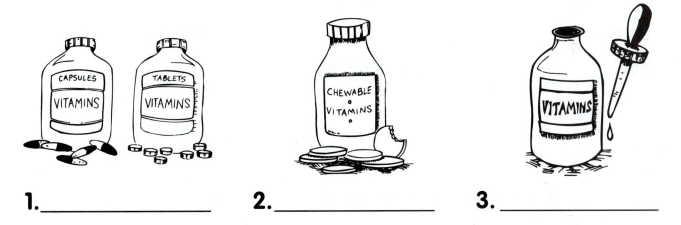

1._____   2._____   3._____

Checklist for Health

☑ what is important for good health.

1. ❏ vitamins

2. ❏ exercise

3. ❏ lots of drinking water

4. ❏ sleep and rest

5. ❏ healthy foods

6. ❏ check-ups

7. ❏ cigarettes

What should they do?

Tam is tired. He _____ exercise everyday, but he _____ rest too. He _____ not smoke cigarettes. He _____ eat good food. Then he _____ feel better.

Fin is pregnant. She _____ go to the doctor. She _____ take vitamins. She _____ rest. She _____ eat healthy food.

1. Should she take vitamins?

_____, _____ _____.

2. Should he stop smoking?

_____, _____ _____.

3. Should she rest?

_____, _____ _____.

4. Should she eat good food?

_____, _____ _____.

5. Should he eat healthy food?

_____, _____ _____.

Complete the sentences with should or shouldn't.

1. I have a fever.

You _____ go to school.

You _____ put on a sweater.

You _____ drink orange juice.

2. I have a cold.

You _____ wear a sweater.

You _____ rest.

You _____ kiss a baby.

3. I feel dizzy.

You _____ rest.

You _____ drive.

You _____ tell your doctor.

4. My eyes are blurry.

You _____ see an eye doctor.

You _____ drive a car.

You _____ read a book.

5. I'm always tired.

You _____ eat healthy food.

You _____ have a check-up.

You _____ stop smoking.

A. Hello. This is

| Miss |
| Mrs. |
| Mr. |
| Ms. |

_____.

I need to make an appointment.

B. That's fine. What for?

A. My

| son |
| daughter |

needs

| a physical. |
| an eye exam. |
| a dental check-up. |

B. Can you come Tuesday the twenty-first at 3:00?

A. Tuesday the twenty-first at 3:00? Yes, I can.

• •

Write the appointment times on the correct dates.

MAY

SUN	MON	TUE	WED	THU	FRI	SAT
			1	2	3	4
5	6	7	8	9	10	11
12	13	14	15	16	17	18
19	20	21	22	23	24	25
26	27	28	29	30	31	

A. He's getting | a physical.
an examination.
a check-up.

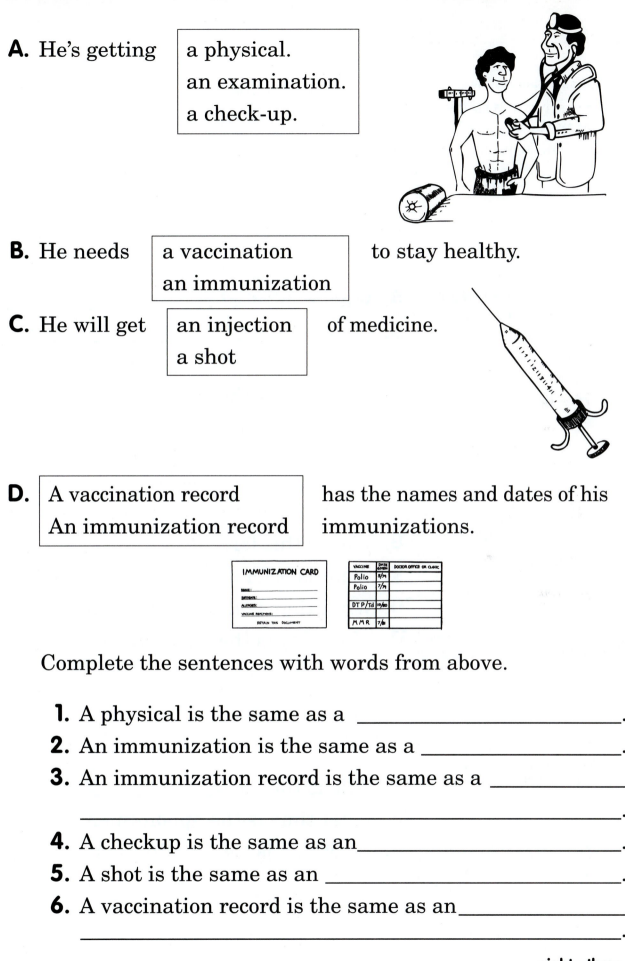

B. He needs | a vaccination
an immunization | to stay healthy.

C. He will get | an injection
a shot | of medicine.

D. | A vaccination record
An immunization record | has the names and dates of his immunizations.

Complete the sentences with words from above.

1. A physical is the same as a _____.

2. An immunization is the same as a _____.

3. An immunization record is the same as a _____

_____.

4. A checkup is the same as an_____.

5. A shot is the same as an _____.

6. A vaccination record is the same as an_____

_____.

```
        Chris
_____
    has an appointment
  ☐M ☐T ☐W ☑Th ☐F
  May 12  at   1:00
      Dr. B. Paul
       555-9981
```

1. Who is this for? _____
2. What time is the appointment? _____
3. What day is the appointment? _____

```
 DENTAL APPOINTMENT
      Dr. North
        Matt
_____
    has an appointment
  ☐M ☑T ☐W ☐Th ☐F
  Dec. 19  at   3:30
```

4. Who is this for? _____
5. What is it for? _____
6. What time is the appointment? _____
7. What day is the appointment? _____

```
  EYE APPOINTMENT
 for  Pat

  ☐M ☐T ☐W ☐Th ☒F
  Jan. 7  at   2:15
Dr. Joan        555-1234
```

8. Who is this for? _____
9. What is it for? _____
10. What time is the appointment? _____
11. What day is the appointment? _____

```
  APPOINTMENT CARD
   L. TURNER, M.D.
        Tony
_____
    has an appointment
 Wed., June 24, 1:45
 date            time
```

12. Who is this for? _____
13. What time is the appointment? _____
14. What day is the appointment? _____

A. Good morning. We need to complete this form.

B. O.K.

A. Have you ever had the chicken pox?

B. Yes, I have.

A. Have you ever had the measles?

B. No, I haven't.

A. Have you ever had heart problems?

B. I'm not sure.

· ·

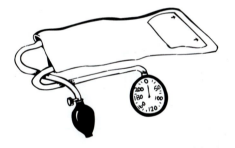

1. Let me take your blood pressure.

2. I want to check your blood pressure.

3. Let me listen to your | heart. lungs. chest. |

4. I want to listen to your | heart. lungs. chest. |

NEW PATIENT FORM

Patient's name: _____

Age _____ Birthdate _____ Sex _____

Patient's address: _____

Please [✓] if you have ever had :

- ❏ chicken pox
- ❏ measles
- ❏ mumps
- ❏ rubella
- ❏ high blood pressure
- ❏ allergies
- ❏ polio
- ❏ TB
- ❏ diabetes

Please [✓] if you have ever been treated for:

- ❏ heart problems
- ❏ lung problems
- ❏ kidney problems
- ❏ other _____
- ❏ liver problems
- ❏ bladder problems
- ❏ stomach problems

Have you ever had an operation? ❏ yes   When? _____
                                 ❏ no   On what? _____

Are you taking medicine now?   ❏ yes
                               ❏ no

Name of medicine _____
Do you have insurance? ❏ yes
                        ❏ no
Name of insurance _____

_____   _____
        Signature   Date

As your classmates: Circle their answers in the correct box.

| Name | Have you ever ever had... | | | |
	chicken pox?	measles?	mumps?	polio?
1.	yes no	yes no	yes no	yes no
2.	yes no	yes no	yes no	yes no
3.	yes no	yes no	yes no	yes no
4.	yes no	yes no	yes no	yes no

1. Who had chicken pox?

_____

2. Who had polio?

_____

3. Who had mumps?

_____

4. Who had measles?

_____

A. What's wrong? You look sick.

B. Oh, I have a headache.

A. Would you like an aspirin?

B. No thanks. I think I'm allergic to aspirin.

A. You should tell your doctor.

I You We They	think

He She	thinks

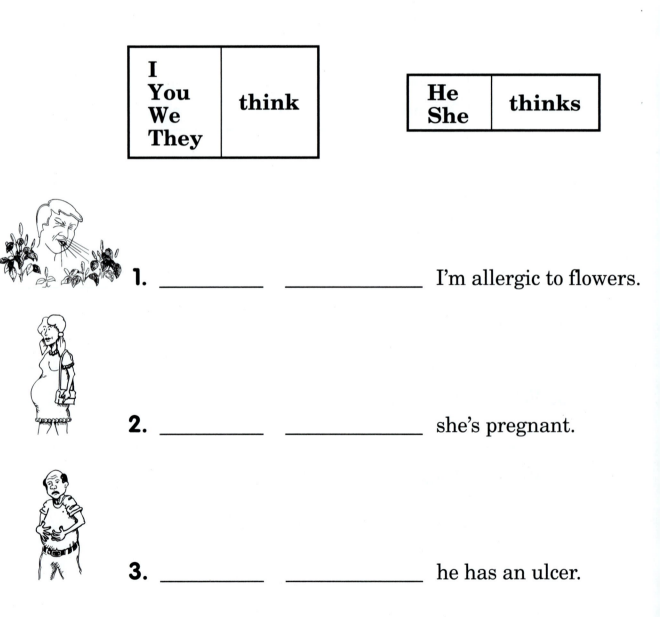

1. _____ _____ I'm allergic to flowers.

2. _____ _____ she's pregnant.

3. _____ _____ he has an ulcer.

A. Do you have any allergies?

B. Yes, I do. I'm allergic to dust. I get really sick.

A. Does he have any allergies?

B. Yes, he does. He's allergic to milk.
He gets a stomachache.

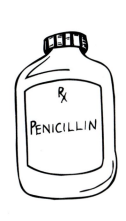

1. _____ 2. _____ 3. _____

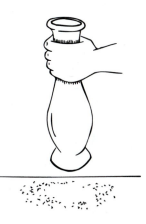

4. _____ 5. _____ 6. _____

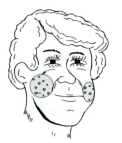

1. He gets a rash.

He _____ allergic to penicillin.

2. She can't breathe.

She _____ allergic to grass.

3. He gets a stomachache.

He _____ _____ to milk.

4. She gets watery eyes and a runny nose.

She _____ _____ to animals.

5. She sneezes.

_____ _____ _____ to dust.

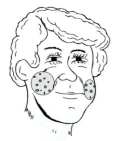

1. He's allergic to penicillin.

He _____.

2. She's allergic to grass and flowers.

She _____.

3. He's allergic to milk.

He _____.

4. She's allergic to animals.

She _____.

5. She's allergic to dust.

She _____.

A. Let's check your blood pressure.

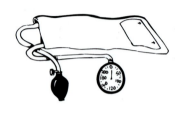

B. O.K. What is it?

A. It's _____ over _____ .

Let's listen to your heart now. Do you smoke?

B. No, I don't.

A. Do you exercise?

B. Yes, I do. I walk every day.

A. Do you eat well?

B. Yes, I do.

A. Do you get enough rest?

B. Yes, I do. I sleep well too.

A. I want a blood and urine sample.

Please go to the lab.

• •

1. What is your blood pressure? _____

2. Do you exercise? _____

3. How many hours do you sleep? _____

```
┌─────────────────────────────────────┐
│            DR. TURNER                │
│  NAME _____ DATE _____  │
│  ADDRESS _____ │
│  PHONE _____ │
│  Rx:  Take one  capsule 4 times      │
│       a day  for  10 days.           │
│                                      │
│              DOCTOR'S SIGNATURE      │
└─────────────────────────────────────┘
```

A. You have an infection. Have you ever had penicillin?

B. I'm not sure.

A. I'm giving you a prescription for penicillin.
Take it four times a day for ten days.

B. How much?

A. One capsule.

B. O.K. One capsule four times a day for ten days.

• •

1. Take it four times a day:
   1. morning
   2. noon
   3. afternoon
   4. night

2. Take it for ten days:

1. Monday	**6.** Saturday
2. Tuesday	**7.** Sunday
3. Wednesday	**8.** Monday
4. Thursday	**9.** Tuesday
5. Friday	**10.** Wednesday

Match

1. teaspoon_____   **a.** twice

2. tablespoon_____   **b.** wk.

3 one time_____   **c.** hrs.

4. hours _____   **d.** once

5. week _____   **e.** Tbl. or T

6. two times_____   **f.** tsp. or t

Write the letters that are underlined to make the abbreviation.

1. <u>teasp</u>oon_____

2. <u>Tabl</u>espoon_____

3. <u>hours</u> _____

4. <u>Doctor</u> _____

5. <u>week</u> _____

1 T.
once a day

How much? _____

When?   _____

2 tsp.
every 4 hrs.

How much? _____

When?   _____

Read the dosage and answer the questions.

2 tsp. every 4 hrs. for 3 days

1. How much? _____

2. When? _____

3. How long? _____

1 capsule every morning for 10 days

4. How much? _____

5. When? _____

6. How long? _____

1 T every 6 hrs. for 1 wk.

7. How much? _____

8. When? _____

9. How long? _____

1 tablet twice a day for 14 days

10. How much? _____

11. When? _____

12. How long? _____

1/2 tsp. in the morning for 10 days

13. How much? _____

14. When? _____

15. How long? _____

3 tsp. 4 times a day for 2 wks.

16. How much? _____

17. When? _____

18. How long? _____

Match

1. generic _____   **a.** be careful

2. dosage_____   **b.** talk to your doctor about this

3. warning _____   **c.** how much medicine you take

4. consult _____   **d.** another name of the medicine

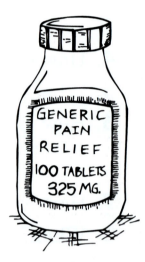

Read the directions from the medicine bottle.

Medicine Directions: Acetaminophen *Dosage:* Adults 1 or 2 tablets every 4-6 hours. Children 6-12 1 tablet. Children under 6 call a doctor. *Warning:* Do not exceed 12 tablets a day. Do not drive if drowsy. Consult your doctor if pregnant.

1. My father has a headache.

    How many tablets should he take? _____

2. My two-year-old daughter has a fever.

    How many should she take? _____

3. His wife has a backache.

    How many should she take? _____

4. My friend has a headache, but she's pregnant.

    How many should she take? _____

A. My ear hurts.

B. How long has it hurt?

A. About one week.

B. You have an ear infection. Are you allergic to any medicine?

A. No, I'm not.

B. Do you take any other medicine?

A. I take vitamins.

Ask your classmates.

Name	Do you take any medicine?	What medicines do you take?	Why do you take it?
1.			
2.			
3.			

DR. TURNER

NAME _____ DATE _____
ADDRESS _____
PHONE _____

R︎: Take one capsule 4 times a day for 10 days.

DOCTOR'S SIGNATURE

A. Did you go to the doctor?

B. Yes, I did.

A. What's the matter?

B. I have an ear infection.

A. Did you get a prescription?

B. Yes. I have to go to the pharmacy now to fill it.

A. How long do you have to take the medicine?

B. I have to take it for ten days. Then I have to see the doctor again.

· ·

have to

1. I have an ear infection.

2. I _____ _____ _____ to the pharmacy.

3. I _____ _____ _____ some medicine.

4. I _____ _____ _____ it for ten days.

5. Then I _____ _____ _____ the doctor again.

Prescriptions

The doctor writes prescriptions. Your prescription for medicine will have your name on it. The doctor will sign it. Sometimes you have to fill in your address and phone number on the prescription. Take the prescription to the pharmacy. The pharmacist fills prescriptions. You have to follow the directions on the prescription.

1. How much do you take?

_____

2. When do you take it?

_____

3. How many days do you take it?

_____

4. Fill in the top part of the prescription with your information.

I You	have to	go to the doctor.
He She It	has to	stay inside. take medicine. get some rest.
We They	have to	drink water.

What do they have to do? Complete the sentences.

1. I have an ear infection.

_____ _____ _____ _____ to the doctor.

_____ _____ _____ _____ medicine.

2. He has a bladder infection.

_____ _____ _____ _____ to the doctor.

_____ _____ _____ _____ medicine.

3. My children have the chicken pox.

_____ _____ _____ _____ inside

_____ _____ _____ _____ some rest.

4. La is pregnant.

_____ _____ _____ _____ the doctor.

_____ _____ _____ _____ some rest.

5. Sam has a fever.

_____ _____ _____ _____ water.

_____ _____ _____ _____ some rest.

A. I need to see the doctor again.

B. When?

A. In ten days.

B. O.K. How is Monday at 9:30?

A. Oh, that's not convenient.

B. O.K. How about Monday at 11:00?

A. That's not convenient either.
Can I come in the afternoon?

B. Let's see. How about Monday at 2:15?

A. O.K. Monday at 2:15 is fine.

· ·

Listen and fill in the information.

1. It's on _____ at _____.

2. It's on _____ at _____.

3. It's on _____ at _____.

4. It's on _____ at _____.

Emergency Room

A. My son stepped on a nail.

B. Has he ever had a tetanus shot?

A. I don't know.

B. It's important. Do you have his immunization record?

A. Yes, I do. Here it is.

B. His tetanus shot was over ten years ago. He needs another one.

....

IMMUNIZATION CARD

NAME: _____

BIRTHDATE: _____

ALLERGIES: _____

VACCINE REACTIONS: _____

RETAIN THIS DOCUMENT

VACCINE	DATE GIVEN	DOCTOR OFFICE OR CLINIC
Polio	5/79	
Polio	7/79	
DTP/Td	10/80	
MMR	7/81	

A. I can't come to school for a few weeks.

B. Oh, why not?

A. I'm going to have an operation.

B. What kind?

A. I'm going to have an eye operation.

B. I hope it's nothing serious.

A. My doctor says it's routine.

B. I'm glad to hear that.

* *

| routine   serious |

1. A checkup is _____.

2. Heart surgery is _____.

3. A cut finger is _____.

4. A blood sample is _____.

5. Cancer surgery is_____.

6. A high fever is_____.

Body Organs

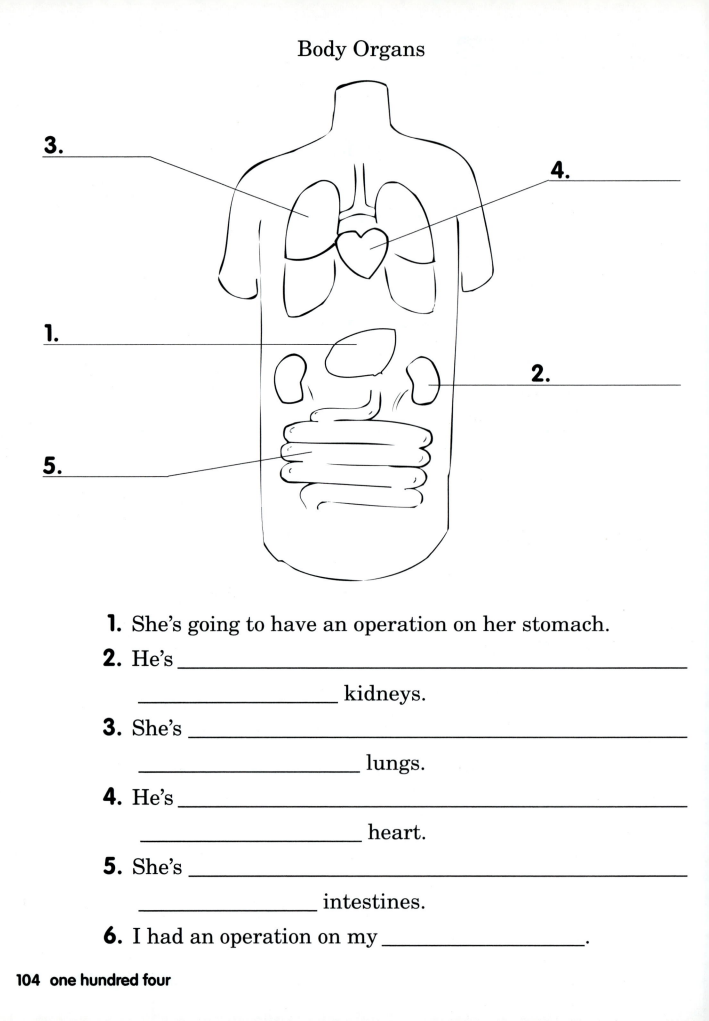

1. She's going to have an operation on her stomach.

2. He's _____
_____ kidneys.

3. She's _____
_____ lungs.

4. He's _____
_____ heart.

5. She's _____
_____ intestines.

6. I had an operation on my _____.

> I'm glad to hear that.
> I'm sorry to hear that.

1. My doctor says it's serious.

_____ _____ _____ _____ _____.

2. My doctor says it's routine.

_____ _____ _____ _____ _____.

3. My friend has a new baby.

_____ _____ _____ _____ _____.

4. My friend is in the hospital.

_____ _____ _____ _____ _____.

5. Her daughter has some cavities.

_____ _____ _____ _____ _____.

6. His daughter has allergies.

_____ _____ _____ _____ _____.

7. Her husband needs an operation.

_____ _____ _____ _____ _____.

8. His son is doing well.

_____.

9. The operation was successful.

_____.

10. The doctor says he can come home.

_____.

Tell the Story.

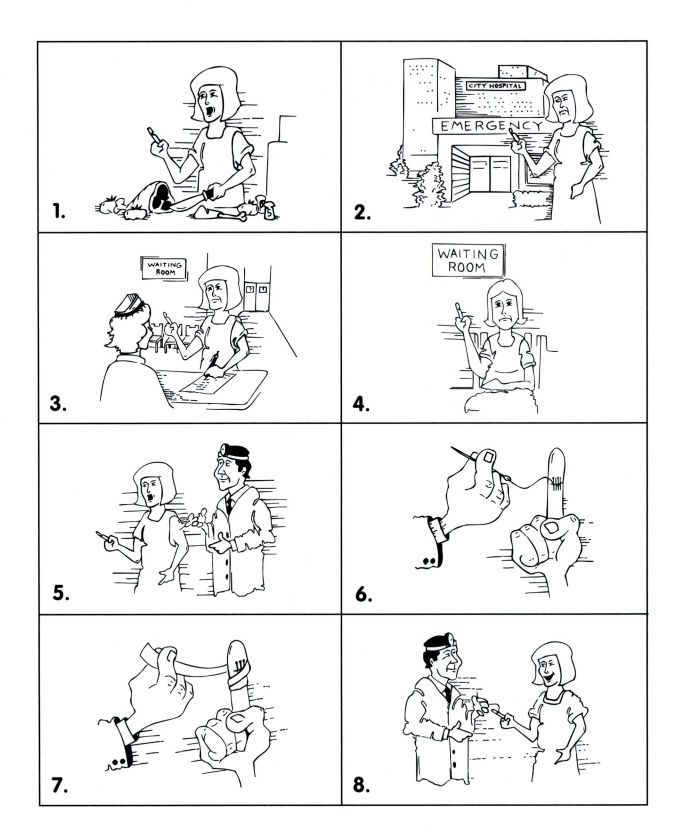

Read the story.

The Emergency Room

Ka cut her finger last week. It was bleeding a lot. She went to the emergency room. The emergency room was very busy. In the emergency room, Ka filled out a medical form. Then she waited to see the doctor. The doctor looked at her finger. He said it was a bad cut. Ka needed a tetanus shot. She needed about ten stitches too. The doctor bandaged her finger to keep it clean. The doctor told Ka to come back in one week. Then he will check her finger again and take out the stitches.

Circle true or false.

1. Ka cut her finger.   true   false

2. Ka went to the doctor's office.   true   false

3. Ka filled out a medical form.   true   false

4. Ka waited a few minutes in the emergency room.   true   false

5. Ka's finger was bleeding a lot.   true   false

6. The nurse bandaged Ka's finger.   true   false

7. The doctor told her to come back in ten days.   true   false

8. Ka will get a tetanus shot in ten days.   true   false

Write the true sentences here.

_____

_____

_____

_____

_____

_____

_____

Answer the questions.

1. Who cut a finger?

_____

2. Where did Ka go?

_____

3. When did she fill out the medical form?

_____

4. What did Ka need?

_____

5. What shot did Ka get? Why?

_____

6. When will Ka go back to the doctor?

_____

7. Why will Ka go back to the doctor?

_____

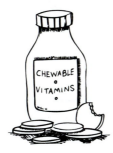

VACCINE	DATE GIVEN	DOCTOR OFFICE OR CLINIC
Polio	5/79	
Polio	7/79	
DTP/Td	10/80	
MMR	7/81	

IMMUNIZATION CARD

NAME: _____

BIRTHDATE: _____

ALLERGIES: _____

VACCINE REACTIONS: _____

RETAIN THIS DOCUMENT

Review the Unit 4 dialogues. Complete the sentences.

1. Sometimes _____ can help you see better.

2. Keep your children's _____ _____ in a safe place.

3. What is your _____ _____?
It's _____ over _____.

4. _____ are important for good health.

5. You have to go to the pharmacy to buy a _____.

6. If you think you are _____ , see a doctor.

7. _____ everyday for good dental health.

5

HOUSING

A. I need a new stove.
B. Why?
A. My old one is broken.
B. Why don't you buy a used one?

1. _____

2. _____

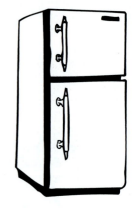

3. _____

4. _____

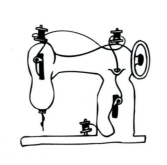

5. _____

6. _____

A. I'm looking for a used TV.
B. I saw one at the thrift store.
A. How much was it?
B. I think it was $75.

· ·

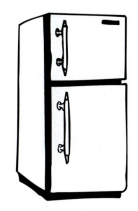

1. I'm looking for a used

_____.

2. _____ _____ _____ _____

_____ garage sale.

3. I'm looking for _____ _____

_____ _____.

4. _____ _____ _____ _____

_____ used furniture store.

5. I'm looking for_____

_____.

6. _____ _____ _____ _____

_____ discount store.

Look for these signs in your neighborhood.

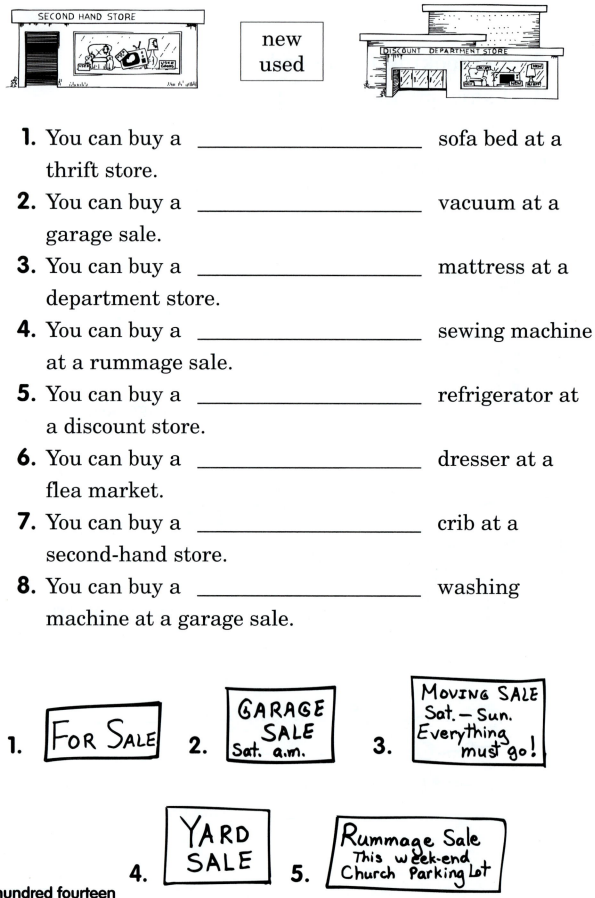

SECOND HAND STORE

new
used

DISCOUNT DEPARTMENT STORE

1. You can buy a _____ sofa bed at a thrift store.

2. You can buy a _____ vacuum at a garage sale.

3. You can buy a _____ mattress at a department store.

4. You can buy a _____ sewing machine at a rummage sale.

5. You can buy a _____ refrigerator at a discount store.

6. You can buy a _____ dresser at a flea market.

7. You can buy a _____ crib at a second-hand store.

8. You can buy a _____ washing machine at a garage sale.

1. FOR SALE

2. GARAGE SALE Sat. a.m.

3. MOVING SALE Sat. — Sun. Everything must go!

4. YARD SALE

5. Rummage Sale This week-end Church Parking Lot

A. How much do you want for the sofa bed?

B. $50.

A. Will you take $40?

B. How about $45?

A. O.K.

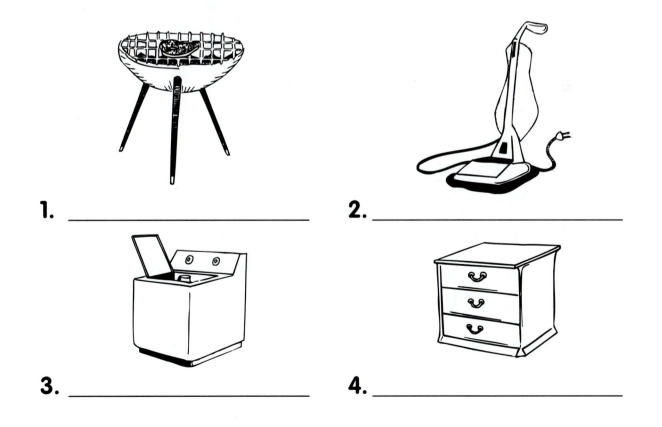

1. _____

2. _____

3. _____

4. _____

A. Can I help you?

B. I saw the vacancy sign. How much is the apartment?

A. It's $925 a month.

B. That's too expensive. Thanks anyway.

A. Can I help you?

B. Do you have an apartment for rent?

A. No, I don't. I can put your name on the waiting list.

B. O.K. Can I fill out the application now?

A. Sure. I'll get it.

Fill out the application.

RENTAL APPLICATION

Name: _____
          Last name   First name

Current address: _____ How long? _____

_____ _____
Number   Street   City   State   Zip code

Previous address: _____ How long? _____

_____ _____
Number   Street   City   State   Zip code

Married ❑   Birthdate: _____
Single ❑
Divorced ❑

How many people are going to live in the apartment? _____

Occupation _____ How long? _____

Name of company _____ (___) _____
                                      Telephone

Address of company _____
                    Number   Street   City   State   Zip code

Monthly income $_____

Name of Bank: _____

Checking ❑ yes ❑ no   Account number _____

Savings   ❑ yes ❑ no   Account number _____

_____ _____
         Signature   Date

Circle yes or no.

1. Did you print your name?   Yes   No

2. Did you write your address?   Yes   No

3. Did you sign your name?   Yes   No

A.

Oak Park, pool
3 Bd. 2 Ba. House
children O.K.
pets O.K.
555-5432

1. How many bedrooms are there? _____
2. How many bathrooms are there? _____
3. Can children live here? _____
4. Is it a house or apartment? _____
5. Can you have pets here? _____

B.

House for rent
Big, clean new
refrigerator, carpet
$875, 4 bd. 1-1/2 ba.
near schools
555-2468

6. How many bedrooms are there? _____
7. How many bathrooms are there? _____
8. How much is the rent? _____
9. Is it a house or apartment? _____
10. Can you have pets here? _____

C.

Denver $825
2 Bd. Apt.,
very clean
No Children
555-1357

11. How many bedrooms are there? _____
12. How many bathrooms are there? _____
13. Can children live here? _____
14. How much is the rent? _____

A, B, or **C**

15. Which one has a pool? _____
16. Which one is near schools? _____
17. Which one has a new refrigerator? _____
18. Which one is an apartment? _____

A. Can I see the apartment for rent?

B. Yes, you can. Let me get the key.

A. How much is the rent?

B. $700 a month.

A. Does the rent include utilities?

B. Only water.

A. Is there a security deposit?

B. Yes, there is. It's $200.

Write the questions.

| Is there a _____ ? |
| Are there _____ ? |

1. _____ security deposit?
2. _____ cleaning deposit?
3. _____ schools near by?
4. _____ rental agreement?
5. _____ parks near by?
6. _____ refrigerator?
7. _____ bus stop near by?
8. _____ laundry room?

| Yes, there is. | No, there isn't. |
| Yes, there are. | No, there aren't. |

Answer the questions.

1. Is there a garage?_____

2. Is there a patio? _____

3. Is there a barbecue on the patio? _____

4. Are there chairs on the patio? _____

5. Is there a table in the kitchen? _____

6. Are there rugs on the floors? _____

7. Is there a sofa in the bedroom? _____

8. Is there a T.V. in the bedroom? _____

9. Is there a laundry room?_____

A. I like this apartment. I want to rent it.

B. Good. You need to pay the first and last month's rent.

A. O.K. Is there a cleaning deposit too?

B. Yes, there is. It's $450.

A. When can I move in?

B. On the fifteenth. Please read the tenant rules.

Read the story.

Moving Day

Today is the first of the month. Thong is very busy this week. He's moving out of his old house. He's moving into a new house. His rent is $750 a month now. It was $825 at his old place. He wants his cleaning deposit back so he has to clean his old house. Moving is a difficult job!

Rules for Tenants

 **1.** Park in numbered space only. Guests park on the street. Don't drive or park on grass.

 **2.** Don't waste water. Don't allow children to play with hoses.

 **3.** Trash pick up is Thursday. Recycle glass, plastic, aluminum, and paper. Put trash in plastic bags or trash cans. Don't put trash in boxes.

 **4.** Don't drop trash on ground. Don't litter.

 **5.** Laundry room is for tenants only. Please use the clothesline or dryer in the laundry room.

 **6.** Don't use barbecue inside. Charcoal is poisonous.

Answer the questions.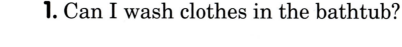

Yes, you can.	
No, you can't.	

1. Can I wash clothes in the bathtub?

_____

2. Can I put my trash in boxes and paper bags?

_____

3. Can I use a barbecue inside my apartment?

_____

4. Can I park on the grass?

_____

5. Can I play in the water?

_____

6. Can I drop my trash on the ground?

_____

A. What's the date?

B. It's _____.

A. When is the rent due?

B. Every month on the first.

A. Do you keep the rent receipts?

B. Yes, I do. I keep them in a box.

· ·

DATE _Sept. 1_ NO _____

RECEIVED OF _M. Turner_____

_750.00_____ DOLLARS

FOR _rent for September 1–30_____

PREVIOUS BALANCE $_____

AMOUNT PAID $_____

BALANCE DUE $_____ BY_____

1. How much is the rent? _____

2. What's the date?_____

3. Who paid? _____

4. What month is it for? _____

A. Did you pay the rent this month?

B. Oh, no! I forgot to pay it. It was due on the fifteenth.

A. Do you have to pay a late charge?

B. Yes. I think it's five dollars.

· ·

Answer the questions.

1. When is your rent due?

_____

2. When is your telephone bill due?

_____

3. When is your gas and electric bill due?

_____

4. When is your water bill due?

_____

5. When is your car payment due?

_____

When is your rent due?

When do you pay it?

Kao's Bad Day

Kao had a bad experience. His rent is due on the first of every month. On the first, he bought a money order, and walked to the manager's office. He wanted to pay his rent. The manager was talking to some new people. He waited to talk to the manager. He waited and waited. The manager said, "Come back later". Kao walked back to his apartment. The next day, Kao went to the office again. He gave the money order to the manager. The manager told him his rent was late. He said Kao needed to pay a late charge. Kao was very confused. He didn't understand what happened. What can he do next time?

Circle true or false.

1.	Kao's rent is due on the fifteenth.	true	false
2.	Kao's rent is due on the first.	true	false
3.	Kao bought a money order to pay his rent.	true	false
4.	The manager was busy in his office.	true	false
5.	The manager said, "Just a minute" to Kao.	true	false
6.	Kao went back to his apartment.	true	false
7.	Kao went to the office the next day.	true	false
8.	Kao didn't have to pay a late charge.	true	false
9.	Kao's rent was one day late.	true	false
10.	Kao doesn't understand "Come back later."	true	false

Write the true sentences.

_____

_____

_____

_____

_____

_____

_____

_____

_____

Answer the questions.

1. When is Kao's rent due?

_____

2. Why did the manager tell Kao to come back later?

_____

3. When did Kao go to pay his rent again?

_____

4. What did the manager say to Kao the next day?

_____

5. Can he pay his rent before the first?

_____

6. Can he mail his rent money to the manager?

_____

7. Can he mail a money order to the manager?

_____

A. What's the matter?

B. I came home from school, and I smelled gas.

A. Did you check the pilot lights?

B. I don't know how.

A. I'm not busy right now. Let me check them.

B. Good. Thanks.

Check in your house or apartment.

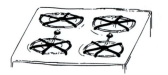

1. Do you have pilot lights in your stove?

_____

2. Do you have a pilot light in your oven?

_____

3. Do you have a pilot light in your heater?

_____

4. Do you have a pilot light in your water heater?

_____

A. Can you check my electricity?

B. What's the problem?

A. The lights aren't working in my bathroom.

B. Did you pay your electric bill?

A. Yes, I did. I have my receipt.

B. I think it's a fuse. I'll come tomorrow.

In case the electricity isn't working, you need:

 **1.** a flashlight

 **2.** batteries

 **3.** candles

 4. matches

5. your manager's phone number

_____

A. What time can you fix my fuse?

B. Later.

A. What time later?

B. Maybe tomorrow.

A. What time tomorrow?

B. In the morning.

A. What time in the morning?

B. 10:00.

A. O.K. I'll see you at 10:00 tomorrow morning.

A. Can you help me write a letter?

B. Sure. What's it about?

A. I want to move next month. I have to give my manager thirty day's notice.

B. O.K. No problem, but remember to make a copy to keep.

....

Sept. 1, 1993

Dear Manager,

This is to inform you that we will move out in 30 days. The address is 9128 Easy Street.

Thank You,

_____

Remember the date, your name, and your address.

	Rent	Utilities	Telephone Bill	Cable TV	Car Insurance	Monthly Total
Tom	$850	$80	$25	$19	$100	
Ann	$825	$75	$17	0	0	
You						

1. Who pays the most rent?_____
2. Who pays the largest phone bill? _____
3. Who pays the most car insurance?_____
4. Who pays the largest utility bill? _____
5. Who pays the most for cable TV? _____
6. What is your largest bill? _____
7. How much does Tom pay monthly? _____
8. How much does Ann pay monthly? _____
9. How much do you pay monthly? _____

May's Budget

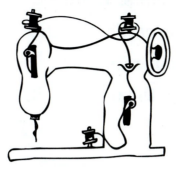

May budgets $1025 a month. Her rent is $525 a month. Her gas and electric bill is $74. Her telephone bill is usually about $18 a month. She pays $50 a month for car gas and $60 a month for car insurance. She pays $250 a month for food. She wants to buy a sewing machine. A used sewing machine will cost about $200. May likes to sew. She can sew her clothes and save money. Maybe she can earn money sewing too. Do you think she can afford the sewing machine?

1. Does May have a lot of money?

_____

2. How much are her bills for one month?

_____

3. How much is the sewing machine?

_____

4. Do you think she can afford the sewing machine?

_____

5. How much can she save a month?

_____

6. How many months will it take to save the money for the sewing machine?

_____

Keep a shoe box for your receipts. Write names of the bills you pay on cards. Put the cards in the box. Keep all your receipts in the box behind the card with the name on it.

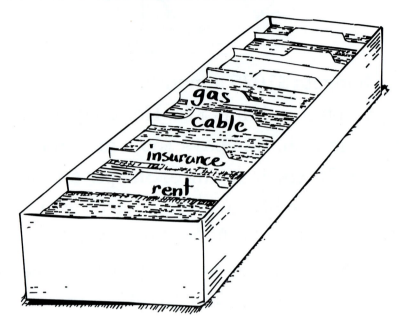

Complete the sentences.

1. May budgets _____ a month.

I budget _____ .

2. Her rent is _____ a month.

My rent is _____ .

3. Her telephone bill is _____ a month.

My phone bill is _____ .

4. Her gas and electric bill is_____ a month.

My gas and electric bill is_____ .

5. She pays _____ for car gas a month.

I pay _____ for gas.

6. She can save _____ a month.

I can save _____ .

7. Write out your budget.

RECEIVED OF _M. Turner_ DATE _Sept 1_ NO ___
_750. 00_ DOLLARS
FOR _rent for September 1-30_
PREVIOUS BALANCE $ _____
AMOUNT PAID $ _____
BALANCE DUE $ _____ BY _____

Sept. 1, 1993

Dear Manager,
    This is to inform you that we will move out in 30 days. The address is 9128 Easy Street.

        Thank You.

        _____

Review the Unit 5 dialogues. Complete the sentences.

1. Do you have to write a _____ to your landlord before you move?

2. In case the electricity isn't working, you need a _____ and _____.

3. If you smell gas, check your _____ _____.

4. You can buy a used refrigerator at a _____ _____.

5. It's important to save your _____ _____.

6. A _____ sign means there is a place for rent.

VACANCY:
3 BEDROOMS
1 BATH

FOR SALE

GARAGE SALE

6

OUR WORLD

A. What country are you from?

B. I'm from Brazil.

A. Where is that?

B. It's in South America.

A. What's your native language?

B. It's Portugese.

A. Can you speak any other languages?

B. Yes, I can. I speak English and _____.

COUNTRY	LANGUAGE	PEOPLE
1. France	French	French
2. United States	English	American
3. Mexico	Spanish	Mexican
4. China	Chinese	Chinese
5. _____	_____	_____
6. _____	_____	_____
7. _____	_____	_____
8. _____	_____	_____

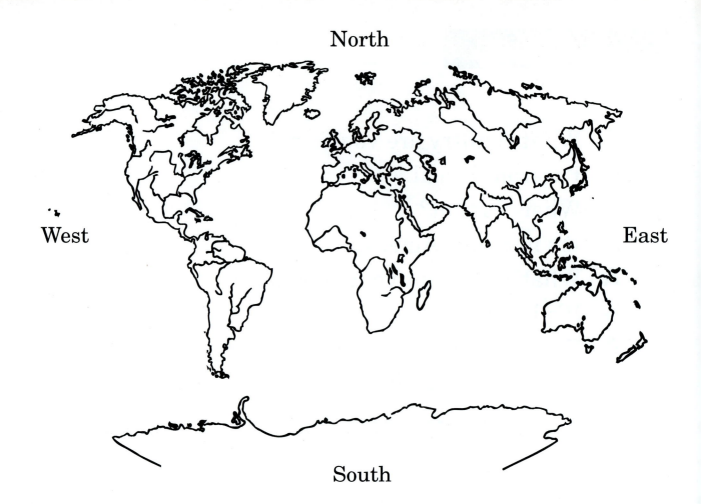

North

West

East

South

This is a map of the world. There are seven continents in the world. The seven continents are, Africa, Asia, Antarctica, Australia, Europe, North America, and South America.

Where is the continent of_____?

1. Africa　　　　　color it green.

2. Asia　　　　　　color it orange.

3. Antarctica　　　color it red.

4. Australia　　　　color it yellow.

5. Europe　　　　　color it purple.

6. North America　color it brown.

7. South America　color it blue.

Ask your classmates.

Name	What country are you from?	Where is it?	What is your native language?
1. Yazmin	Peru	South America	Spanish
2.			
3.			
4.			

Use the chart to write sentences about your classmates.

1. Yazmin is from Peru. Peru is in South America.
   Her native language is Spanish.

2. _____

   _____

3. _____

   _____

4. _____

   _____

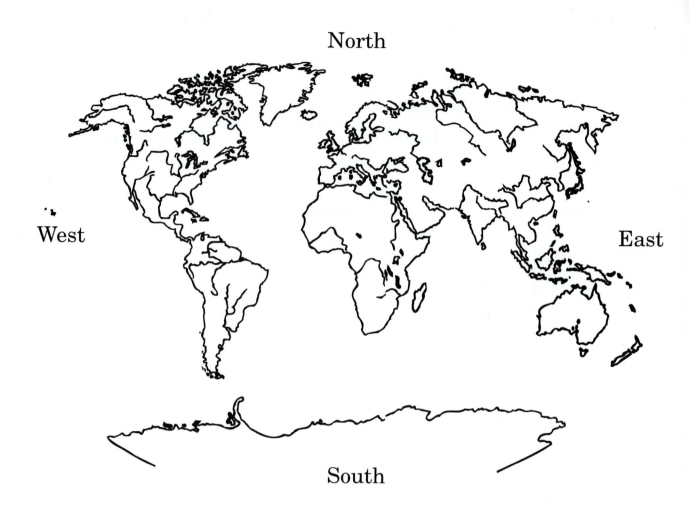

North

West

East

South

Complete the sentences with north, south, east or west.

1. The sun comes up in the _____.

2. The sun sets in the _____.

3. The continent of Antarctica is in the _____.

4. The continent of Asia is in the_____.

5. The Pacific Ocean is_____of the U.S.

6. The Atlantic Ocean is _____of the U.S.

7. The continent of Europe is _____of Africa.

8. The continent of Australia is_____of Asia.

9. My native country is _____of the U.S.

1.

2.

3.

4.

5.

6.

7.

8.

9.

10.

11.

12.

A. Tell me about your native country.

B. It's beautiful.

A. Did you live in | a city?
the countryside?

B. _____.

A. Did you live near | a river?
a lake?
an ocean?

B. _____.

A. Are there a lot of | mountains?
trees?
animals?
people?
cars?

B. _____.

A. Is the weather | hot?
cold?
rainy?
dry?
humid?

B. _____.

A. Are you homesick sometimes?

B. _____.

Answer the questions about your native country in complete sentences.

1. What country are you from?

_____

2. Where is it?

_____

3. What is the capital of your native country?

_____

4. Who is the leader of your native country?

_____

5. What is the main industry in your native country?

_____

6. What is the largest river in your native country?

_____

7. How is the weather in your native country?

_____

Write your answers to make a story about your native country.

MY NATIVE COUNTRY

_____

_____

_____

_____

_____

_____

_____

_____

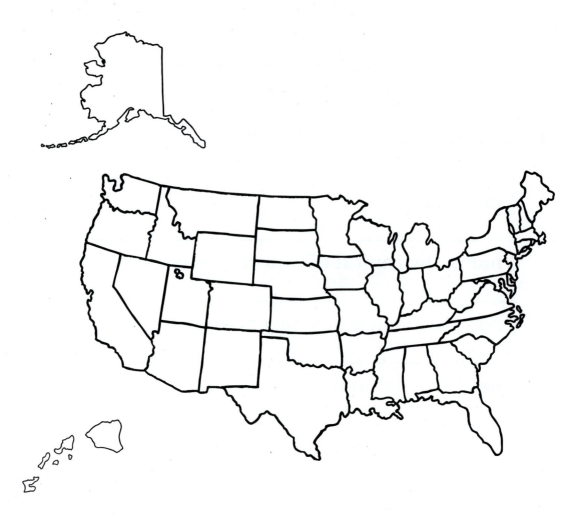

This is the United States. It has fifty states. Washington, D.C., is the capital of the United States. The President lives in Washington, D.C.

Can you find _____?

1. Washington D.C.   Put a ✳ on it.
2. California   Put a ✔ on it.
3. Alaska   Put a ⬤ on it.
4. Virginia   Put a ✚ on it.
5. your state   Put an ✘ on it.

Washington D.C.

The capital of the United States is Washington, D.C. Washington, D.C. is not a state, but it is a very important city. The "D" is for district. The "C" is for Columbia. Washington, D.C. is another name for the District of Columbia. It is between the states of Maryland and Virginia. The President of the United States lives in the White House in Washington, D.C. The Capitol Building is also in Washington, D.C.

1. What is the capital of the United States?

_____

2. Who lives in Washington, D.C.?

_____

3. What is another name for Washington, D.C.?

_____

4. Where is Washington, D.C.?

_____

5. What famous buildings are in Washington, D.C.?

_____

6. Is Washington, D.C. a city or a state?

_____

A. What state do you live in now?

B. _____

A. What city?

B. _____

A. What's the capital of your state?

B. _____

A. What other states have you lived in?

B. _____

A. What other states have you visited?

B. _____

• •

There are fifty states in the United States. Each state has a capital city. The governor of the state lives in the capital city. Each state has a special flag, a special name, and a special flower. Write about your state here.

1. I live in _____ (state).

2. The state capital is _____.

3. The special name of my state is _____.

4. My state flower is _____.

5. The colors of my state flag are _____.

6. The governor of my state is _____.

Three things I like about my new country are:

1. _____

_____ .

2. _____

_____ .

3. _____

_____ .

Three things I miss about my native country are:

1. _____

_____ .

2. _____

_____ .

3. _____

_____ .

A. How did you come to the U.S.A.?

B. First I took a bus to the airport.
Then I flew to Japan.
Next I flew to San Francisco.
Then my brother drove me here.
How about you?

A. Well, first I _____

_____

_____

_____

_____

• •

1. I drove.

2. I walked.

3. I flew.

4. I took a boat.

5. I took a bus.

A. When did you come to the U.S.?

B. I came in 1993.

A. How did you come?

B. I flew to New York. Then I took a bus here.

A. Where did you live before?

B. I lived in

| another country.
| another state.
| another city.
| a refugee camp.

A. When did you start school here?

B. I started school here in September 1993.

· ·

What's the past tense of these words?

1. come   _____

2. fly   _____

3. take   _____

4. live   _____

5. start   _____

6. go   _____

7. drive   _____

8. arrive   _____

As your classmates:

Name	When did you come?	How did you come?	Where did you live before?	When did you start school?
1.				
2.				
3.				
4.				

Use the chart to write sentences about yourself and your classmates.

_____

_____

_____

_____

_____

_____

_____

Name	When did you come?	How did you come?	Where did you live before?	When did you start school?
Kim	May 1992	plane	Philippines	Sept. 1992
Farida	March 1993	plane	Afganistan	April 1993
Faustino	Oct. 1991	bus	Guatemala	Jan. 1992

Use the chart to answer the questions.

1. Who came to the U.S. in 1993?

_____

2. When did Faustino start school here?

_____

3. How did Farida and Kim come here?

_____

4. How did Faustino come here?

_____

5. Where did Farida live before?

_____

6. Where did Kim live before?

_____

Interview your classmates.

Name	When were you born?	When did you get married?	When did you have your first child?	When did you leave your native country?	When did you come to the U.S.?	When did you start school?
1. May	1949	1965	1967	1980	1982	1984
2.						
3.						
4.						

Write six sentences about one of your classmates.

_____

_____

_____

_____

_____

_____

Share this story with your classmates.

Tell the Story

1.

2.

3.

4.

5.

6.

Anna's Story

Anna was born in Poland in 1961. She got married in 1981. She had her first child in 1984. Her husband came to the United States in 1989. She came to the U.S. with their child in 1993. She started school in 1994. She wants to become a citizen. She's learning the Pledge of Allegiance now.

Complete Anna's timeline.

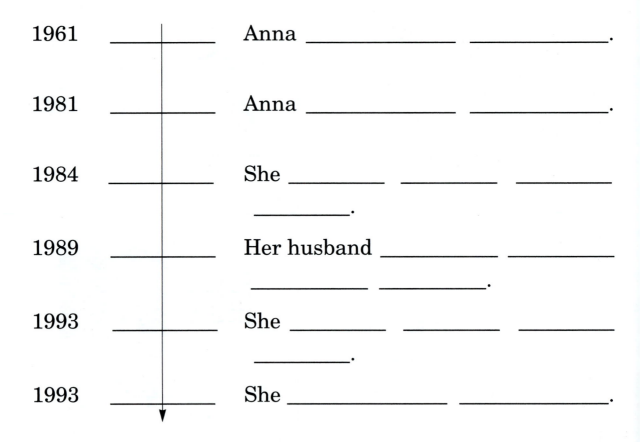

1961 _____|_____ Anna _____ _____.

1981 _____|_____ Anna _____ _____.

1984 _____|_____ She _____ _____ _____
_____.

1989 _____|_____ Her husband _____ _____
_____ _____.

1993 _____|_____ She _____ _____ _____
_____.

1993 _____|_____ She _____ _____.

Write about Yourself

_____ Story

I was born in_____ in_____.

I got married in _____ . I had my first child in

_____ . I came to the U.S. in_____.

I started school in_____.

Complete your own timeline.

DATE   WHAT HAPPENED?

_____   I was born.

The Pledge of Allegiance

This is the Pledge of Allegiance. We say this pledge at many school functions. When people become citizens of the United States, they say the Pledge.

I pledge allegiance to the flag of the United States of America and to the republic for which it stands, one nation, under God, indivisible, with liberty and justice for all.

This is the flag of the United States. It's red, white, and blue. It has thirteen stripes and fifty stars. There is one stripe for each of the first thirteen states. There is one star for each of the fifty states.

1. This is the flag of _____ _____
_____. It's red, white, and blue. It has
thirteen _____ and fifty _____ on it.

Draw the flag of your native country.

2. This is the flag of my native country, _____
It's _____

Review Unit 6. Complete the sentences.

1. I'm living in the U.S., and I'm studying_____
in school now.

2. The _____ of the U.S. has fifty stars and
thirteen stripes.

3. The President of the U.S. lives in _____.

4. I live in _____.

5. My native country is _____.

6. My native language is _____.

7

TRANSPORTATION

A. Don't cross in the middle of the street.

B. Why not?

A. It's illegal. You can get a ticket.
Cross at the corner or at the light.

B. O.K. Let's cross now. The light says walk.

Number **1** is a _____.

Number **2** is the _____ _____ _____ _____.

Number **3** is a_____ or _____.

1.

2.

3.

4.

5.

6.

7.

8.

9.

10.

11.

12.

A. How do I get to city hall?

B. Take Highway 5 north. Take the Noel Road exit. Go west on Noel Road.

A. How long does it take to get there?

B. It takes about fifteen minutes.

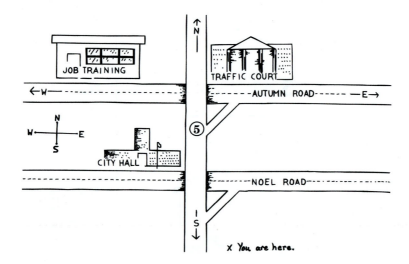

How do I get to traffic court?

1. Take _____ _____ _____ .

2. Take _____ _____ _____ _____ .

3. Go _____ _____ _____ _____ .

How do I get to the job training center?

4. _____ .

5. _____ .

6. _____ .

1. How long does it take to get to the post office?
It takes about _____ minutes.

2. How long does it take to get to the clinic?
It takes about _____ _____.

3. How long does it take to get to the laundromat?
It takes_____ _____ _____.

4. How long does it take to get to the pharmacy?
It _____ _____ _____ _____.

5. How long does it take to get to city hall?
_____ _____ _____ _____ _____.

6. How long does it take to get to the D.M.V.?
_____ _____ _____ _____ _____.

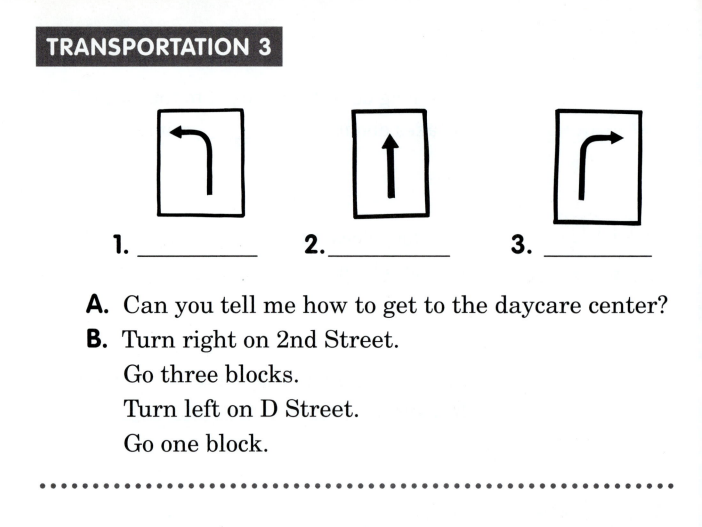

1. _____ 2. _____ 3. _____

A. Can you tell me how to get to the daycare center?

B. Turn right on 2nd Street.

Go three blocks.

Turn left on D Street.

Go one block.

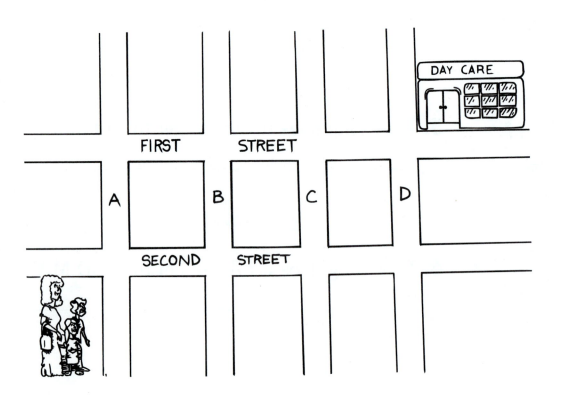

A. Can you give me directions to your house?

B. Sure. Go to _____

_____

_____

_____

_____

A. What's the address?

B. It's _____.

A. How long does it take to get there?

B. It takes about _____ minutes.

· ·

Turn right   Turn left

Listen and fill in.

1. Go _____ blocks. Turn _____.

2. Turn _____ on Second Avenue.

3. Go _____ blocks. Turn_____. Go _____block.

4. Turn _____ on Park Street. Go_____ blocks.

5. Turn _____ on State Street. Go _____ blocks.
Turn _____.

6. Turn _____. Then turn _____ again.

| always | usually | sometimes | never |

Coming to School

Al usually walks to school. It always takes about twenty minutes to walk. Sometimes his friend drives him to school, but Al never drives. Sometimes he takes the bus. The bus is always on time. Al always thinks about buying a car. Then he will drive his friend to school too.

Answer the questions.

1. When does Al take the bus to school?

_____

2. When does Al walk to school?

_____

3. When does Al drive to school?

_____

4. When does Al go to school with a friend?

_____

5. What does Al always think about?

_____

When do they come to school?

	Monday	Tuesday	Wednesday	Thursday	Friday
Maria	☀	☀	☀	☀	☀
Anna	☀		☀		☀
Omar		☀	☀	☀	☀
Tai					

Answer the questions.

1. Does Maria always come to school?

_____

2. Does Omar usually come to school?

_____

3. Does Tai always come to school?

_____

4. When does Anna come to school?

_____

5. When does Omar come to school?

_____

6. When does Tai come to school?

_____

7. When do you come to school?

_____

```
←———————         ———————→
GATES 5-9       GATES 10-15
PAL AIRLINES    LUGGAGE CLAIM
SNACK BAR       RESTROOMS
```

A. Can you tell me where PAL Airlines is?

B. Go straight to the telephones, and turn left.

A. Oh, I see the sign now. Thanks.

• •

Unscramble the questions.

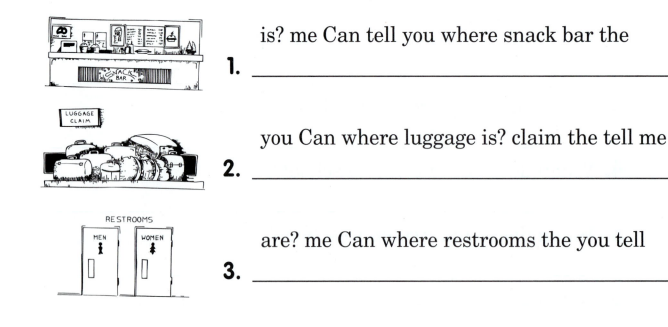

is? me Can tell you where snack bar the

1. _____

you Can where luggage is? claim the tell me

2. _____

are? me Can where restrooms the you tell

3. _____

TICKET COUNTER

PAL AIRLINES

A. Here's my ticket.

B. Do you have any luggage?

A. Yes, I do.

B. Let's check it in. What about that box?

A. I'm going to carry it on.

B. O.K. Go to gate 15 to board.

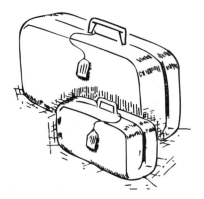 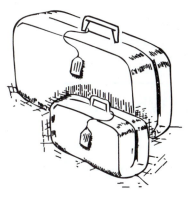

1. _____ or _____

A. Where do I meet flight 10 from Hawaii?

B. It's arriving at gate 7.

A. Is it on time?

B. No, it's delayed.

Flight number	Arriving from	Gate	Time	
789	Dallas	12	7:16 P.M.	arrived
20	New York	19	10:00 A.M.	on time
10	Hawaii	7	2:30	delayed
5	Mexico City	22	8:05	on time

1. Where do I meet flight 20 from New York?

_____

2. Where do I meet flight 5 from Mexico City?

_____

3. Where do I meet flight 789 from Dallas?

_____

Answer the questions.

1. Flight 10 should arrive at 2:30.
It's one hour late. What time will it arrive?_____

2. Flight 21 should arrive at 12:30.
It's three hours late. What time will it arrive? _____

3. Flight 57 should arrive at 4:00.
It's one and a half hours late. What time will it arrive?_____

4. Flight 14 should arrive at 10:00.
It's twenty-five minutes late. What time will it arrive? _____

5. Flight 99 should arrive at 7:45.
It's thirty minutes late. What time will it arrive? _____

6. Flight 38 should arrive at 8:45.
It's on time. What time will it arrive?_____

Tell the story.

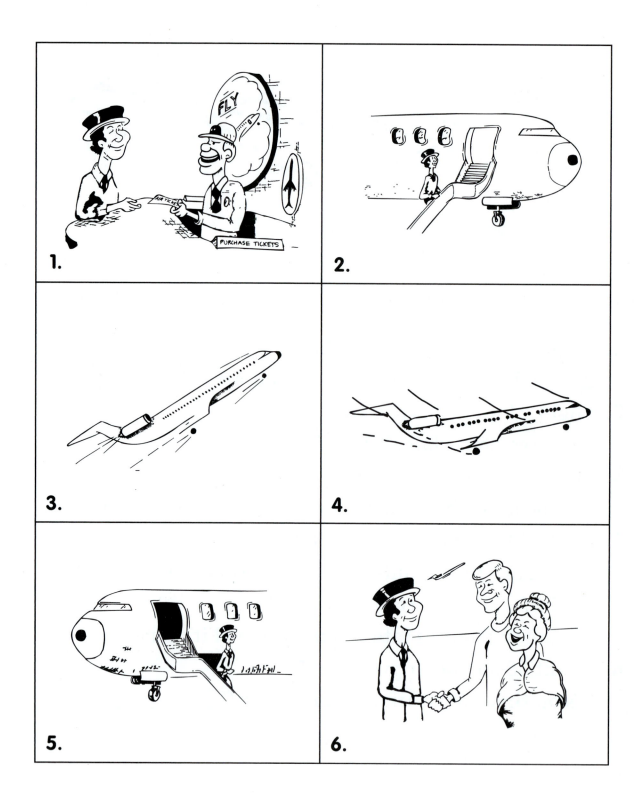

1.

2.

3.

4.

5.

6.

Read the story.

Bob Goes to New York

Bob has friends in New York City. They can help him find a job there. He bought an airplane ticket to New York City. He went to the airport and checked in at the ticket counter. He took all his clothes in his luggage. He checked in his luggage too. The man at the ticket counter said to go to gate fifteen. The plane was leaving soon. Bob walked to gate fifteen. Then he boarded the plane. He sat down and put on his seat belt. The plane took off for New York City. Soon it landed there. It was a good flight. He got his luggage and met his friends. Bob will have a new start. Good luck, Bob.

Circle true or false.

1. Bob has friends in New York City.   true   false

2. Bob's family can help him get a job in
New York City.   true   false

3. Bob needs a job.   true   false

4. Bob went to the airport to take a plane
to New York.   true   false

5. He boarded the plane at gate five.   true   false

6. He met his friends at the airport.   true   false

Write the true sentences.

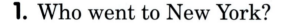

Answer the questions.

1. Who went to New York?

_____

2. How did he go there?

_____

3. Why did Bob go to New York?

_____

4. Who did Bob meet at the airport?

_____

5. How was his flight?

_____

6. Where did the plane land?

_____

7. Did you take a plane?

_____

8. Where did you go?

_____

Car for Sale
runs good
call 555-3192

A. Hello.

B. Hello. I'm calling about the car for sale.

A. Yes.

B. How much is it?

A. It's $1800.

B. What year?

A. '84.

B. What make?

A. Chevrolet.

B. How many miles does it have?

A. 90,000.

B. How are the tires?

A. They're O.K.

Chevy Van '79 new tires $4,000 Automatic 555-1589	1. What year is it? _____
	2. What make is it? _____
	3. How much is it? _____

'82 Honda
air 5 speed
Xlnt condition
555-1035

4. What year is it? _____
5. What make is it? _____
6. Does it have air conditioning? _____

Ford Wagon
'71 runs O.K.
rebuilt engine
$700 555-7798

7. What year is it? _____
8. What make is it? _____
9. How does it run? _____

Toyota Sedan '87
good condition
4 door 4 speed
air 555-7281

10. What year is it? _____
11. What make is it? _____
12. What's the phone number? _____

'93 Nissan truck
like new
555-4884
call after 5 p.m.

13. What year is it? _____
14. What make is it? _____
15. When can you call? _____

A. What condition is the car in?

B. It's in good condition.

A. Can I come and see it this afternoon?

B. Yes. I'll be home after 2:00.

A. O.K. I'll come at 3:00. Can I take it for a test drive?

B. O.K.

1. _____

2. _____

3. _____

4. _____

1. What make is the pick-up? _____

2. What make is the van? _____

3. What make is the station wagon? _____

Chevrolet	Toyota	Ford
1992	1982	1989
$11,500	$1,200	$8,900
25,000	117,000	68,000

4. Which one is the cheapest? _____

5. Which one is the most expensive? _____

6. Which one is the newest? _____

7. Which one is the oldest? _____

8. Which one has the most miles? _____

9. Which one has the least miles? _____

10. Which one do you want to buy? _____

A. How much do you want for your car?

B. I want $1800.

A. Will you take $1500?

B. I'll take $1700.

A. $1650?

B. O.K.

A. Will you take a check?

B. No, I won't. Cash only.

· ·

JOE DOE   101
123 FIRST AVE.
U.S. AMERICA 10011   DATE _____

PAY TO THE ORDER OF _____

_____ DOLLARS

JG BANK   SIGNATURE

1. Will he take a check?

_____

2. Will he take cash?

_____

How much	do does	we they you he she	want for	our their your his her	car?

Write the questions.

1. (you) How much _____car?

2. (Juan) How much _____van?

3. (Habib and Mary) How much _____
_____station wagon.

4. (Anya) How much _____car?

5. (Toan) How much _____truck?

6. (you and I) How much _____
_____van?

7. (Mrs. North) How much _____
_____car?

8. (Mr. and Mrs. Garcia) How much_____
_____station wagon?

9. (Toi, Paul, and I) How much _____
_____pick up truck?

Listen and write the amounts.

1. _____   **3.** _____   **5.** _____

2. _____   **4.** _____   **6.** _____

1.

2.

3.

4.

5.

6.

7.

8.

9.

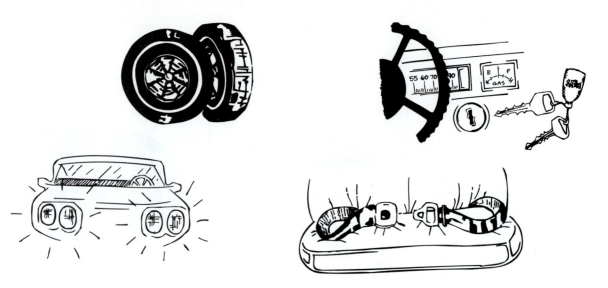

Review Unit 7. Complete the sentences.

1. The car has a flat _____.

2. Everyone should wear _____in the car.

3. Put the key in the _____to start the car.

4. When it is raining, turn on the _____.

5. The car won't go. The _____is empty.

6. Remember to turn on the _____at night.

7. The car won't start. The _____is dead.

8. You can't see if the _____is dirty.

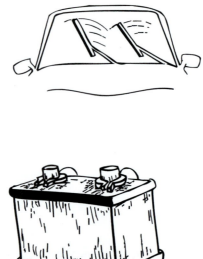

8

EMERGENCIES

A. Did you hear about the earthquake?

B. Yes, I did. It was terrible.

A. The newspaper says there will always be earthquakes.

B. That's bad news.

A. But there is good news. Every day scientists are learning more about earthquakes.

Do you have _____ in your native country?

1. _____

2. _____

3. _____

4. _____

TIMES

• FINAL EDITION •   • FINAL EDITION •

GOOD NEWS	BAD NEWS
1.	1.
	2.
2.	3.
3	4.

Is it good news or bad news? Write the news item under the correct title.

Bit Earthquake in Mexico   Missing Boy Come Home

Car Accident Hurts Three   Police Get Purse Snatcher

Hurricane Comes to Florida   Family Saved from Fire

In case of emergencies, you should have these in your home:

Do you have a radio with batteries?

1. _____

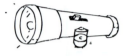
Do you have a flashlight with batteries?

2. _____

Do you have enough prescription medicine?

3. _____

Do you have extra water in bottles?

4. _____

Do you have extra cans of food?

5. _____

Do you have emergency telephone numbers by your phone?

6. _____

EMERGENCY PHONE NUMBERS

POLICE _____

FIRE _____

DOCTOR _____

NEIGHBOR _____

Police.   Can you tell me what happened?

B.   A man stole my purse.

Police.   Where were you?

B.   In the parking lot.

Police.   Are you hurt?

B.   I'm O.K.

Police.   We need to fill out a report.

B.   I speak _____.

Police.   I'll call a translator.

• •

1. What happened here.

_____

_____

2. What happened here?

_____

_____

A. I'm calling to report that somebody robbed my house. My TV is missing.

B. Is there someone in the house now?

A. No.

B. What else is missing?

A. I don't know. I have to check.

B. Don't touch anything. The police will come soon.

· ·

What's the non-emergency police number in your area?

_____

Is it an emergency or non-emergency?

1. Your car is stolen. _____

2. Somebody is throwing rocks at children. _____

3. Your neighbors' T.V. is too loud. _____

4. Somebody has a gun outside your home. _____

5. Your dog is missing. _____

I'm calling to report that

1. _____ _____ _____ _____
   _____ my car is missing.

2. _____ _____ _____ _____
   _____ somebody broke my window.

3. _____ _____ _____ _____
   _____ somebody stole my purse.

4. _____ _____ _____ _____
   _____ somebody beat up my son.

5. _____ _____ _____ _____
   _____ my neighbors are fighting.

6. _____ _____ _____ _____
   _____ somebody tried to kidnap
   my children.

In an emergency I have to:

1. STAY CALM

2. GET HELP

3. WAIT FOR THE POLICE

I	have to
He She It	has to
We You They	have to

1. My car is missing. I _____ _____ call the police.

2. Somebody stole her purse. She _____ _____ call the police.

3. Somebody beat up our son. We _____ _____ take him to the doctor.

4. Somebody broke his window. He _____ _____ call his landlord.

5. My neighbors are fighting. I _____ _____ call the police.

6. Their children said a man was watching them. They _____ _____ call the police.

A. Let's fill out this police report.

B. O.K.

A. What's missing?

B. My color TV.

A. What brand?

B. I don't remember.

A. What color?

B. Brown.

A. How much did it cost?

B. About $200

Match

1. item_____   **a.** color and brand

2. description_____   **b.** the cost

3. value_____   **c.** what is missing

Fill in the Police Report

POLICE REPORT

NAME	DATE
ADDRESS	DATE OF BURGLARY
TELEPHONE	TIME OF BURGLARY

HOW MANY ITEMS WERE STOLEN? _____

WHAT IS THE VALUE OF THE ITEMS? _____

What's missing?	What brand?	What color?	How much did it cost?
1.	SANYO		
2.	SCHWINN		
3.	TIMEX		
4.	SEARS		

A. Help please! My son is missing.

B. How long has he been missing?

A. About two hours.

B. What's his name?

A. Raul Vega.

B. Spell that.

A. R - A - U - L   V - E - G - A

B. Does he speak English?

A. Yes, he does.

B. Stay calm. Don't leave your house.
A police officer will come soon.

• •

Could you spell that please?

A as in _____   G as in _____

B as in _____   H as in _____

C as in _____   I as in _____

D as in _____   J as in _____

E as in _____   K as in _____

F as in _____   L as in _____

A. What does he look like?

B. He's about four feet tall. He's thin. He has curly black hair. He has brown eyes.

A. What was he wearing?

B. He was wearing blue jeans, a brown sweater, and white tennis shoes.

A. How old is he?

B. He's seven years old.

A. Did you talk to his friends?

B. Yes, I did. He's not with his friends.

· ·

Could you spell that please?

M as in _____   T as in _____

N as in _____   U as in _____

O as in _____   V as in _____

P as in _____   W as in _____

Q as in _____   X as in _____

R as in _____   Y as in _____

S as in _____   Z as in _____

Match the Opposites

1. young _____	**a.** short _____
2. light _____	**b.** thin _____
3. heavy _____	**c.** dark _____
4. tall _____	**d.** short _____
5. long _____	**e.** old _____

1. What does she look like?

She's _____ (young or old)

She's _____ (tall or short).

She has _____ (light or dark) hair.

2. What does he look like?

He's _____.

He's _____.

He has _____.

3. What does she look like?

_____

_____

I He She	was	
You We They	were	wearing...

1. What was he wearing?

_____ _____ _____ jeans,

a dark sweater, and white shoes.

2. What was she wearing?

_____ _____ _____ _____

_____

_____

3. What were you wearing yesterday?

_____

_____

A. _____ can't come to school today.

B. Why? What happened?

A. He was in a car accident.

B. Oh no! How is he?

A. He has a broken leg.

B. Was he wearing a seat belt?

A. Yes, he was.

B. Does he have insurance?

A. Yes, he does. But it wasn't his fault.

· ·

1.    He was hit from behind.
He was rear-ended.

2.   He was hit head on.

A. Oh no. That car hit the little boy.
B. It's a hit-and-run. Get the license number.
A. O.K. I'll call the police too. You help the boy.

LICENSE
733 MFR

1. What's the license plate number?

_____

LICENSE
ABC123

2. What's the license plate number?

_____

UR·4·ME

3. What's the license plate?

_____

GO·4·IT

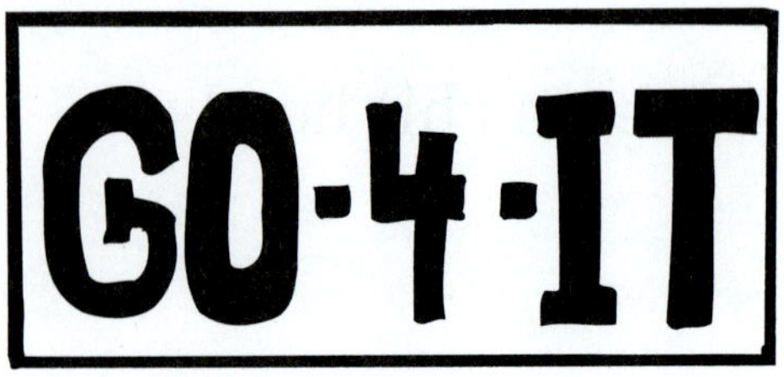

4. What's the license plate?

_____

If you are in a car accident you need to:

1. make sure everyone is O.K.

2. call the police.

3. exchange phone numbers.

4. exchange driver's license numbers.

5. exchange insurance company names.

6. wait for the police to come.

7. _____

If someone is hurt you need to:

1. Cover the injured person with a blanket or jacket.

2. Stay calm, get help, and tell the person that help is coming.

What's the telephone number?

1. Emergency police _____

2. Emergency fire _____

3. Emergency accident _____

4. Poison control center_____

5. Non-emergency police_____

6. Non-emergency fire _____

7. Hospital emergency room _____

8. Gas and electric emergency turn-off _____

9. Food stamp office _____

10. Health clinic _____

11. My doctor _____

12. My school _____

13. My landlord_____

14. My friend _____

A. Poison control center.

B. My daughter ate some aspirin.

A. How old is she?

B. Two and a half.

A. How much does she weigh?

B. About thirty pounds.

A. How many did she take?

B. Ten or twelve.

A. What time did this happen?

B. Fifteen minutes ago.

A. Is she conscious?

B. Yes, she is.

A. Take her to the nearest emergency room.

1. He's _____.

2. He's_____.

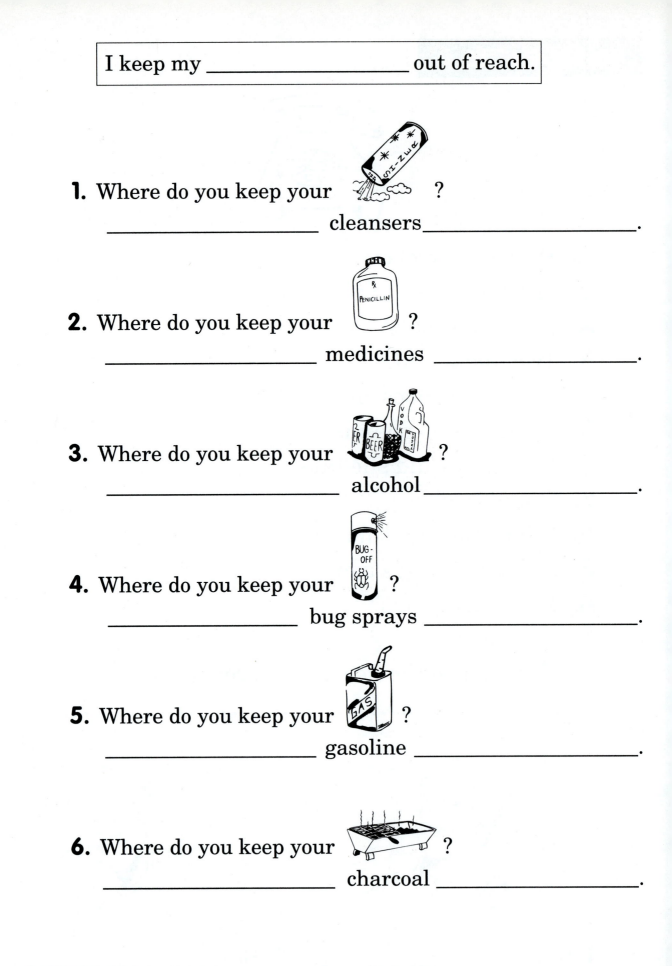

I keep my _____ out of reach.

1. Where do you keep your   ?

_____ cleansers _____.

2. Where do you keep your   ?

_____ medicines _____.

3. Where do you keep your   ?

_____ alcohol _____.

4. Where do you keep your   ?

_____ bug sprays _____.

5. Where do you keep your   ?

_____ gasoline _____.

6. Where do you keep your   ?

_____ charcoal _____.

A. I had a fire in my house yesterday.

B. What happened?

A. The toaster caught on fire. The kitchen was full of smoke.

B. Was anybody hurt?

A. No. The smoke detector warned us early.

What happened?

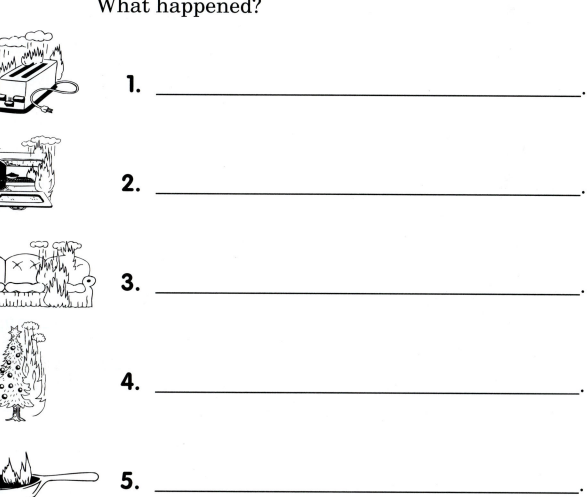

1. _____.

2. _____.

3. _____.

4. _____.

5. _____.

Read the Story

A Thief in the Day

Last week somebody climbed upstairs and went into Pat's apartment. Pat's daughter was at school. Pat was at work. A neighbor saw the man. The thief had long dark hair. He was wearing jeans, a striped shirt, and a baseball cap. He had a handkerchief over his face. He stole about fifteen cassettes, a cassette player, and a box of jewelry. Pat was very afraid but she didn't call the police. She was too afraid to sleep. She was too afraid to go to work the next day. She was worried about her daughter, herself, and her home. What should she do?

She should...

1. _____ call the police.

2. _____ lock all the windows and doors.

3. _____ tell the landlord or manager.

4. _____ warn her neighbors.

5. _____

   _____

Answer the questions.

1. Who saw the thief?

_____

2. What was he wearing?

_____

3. What did he look like?

_____

4. When did this happen?

_____

5. What did he steal?

_____

6. Where was Pat?

_____

7. Where was Pat's daughter?

_____

8. Why was Pat afraid to sleep?

_____

9. Why should Pat call the police?

_____

SIGNS

1. DANGER

2. FIRE ALARM

3. NO TRESPASSING

4. POISON

5. FLAMMABLE

6. HIGH VOLTAGE

7. WARNING

8. FIRE ESCAPE

9. BEWARE OF DOG

10. KEEP OUT

11. FIRE EXTINGUISHER

12. CAUTION

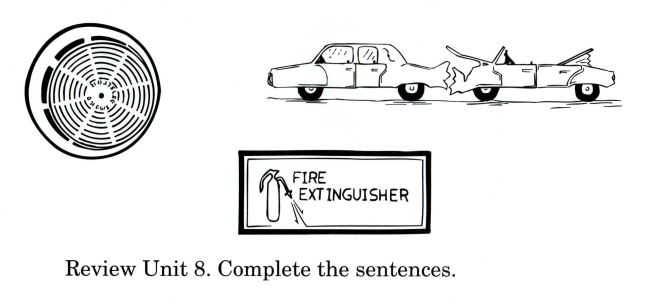

Review Unit 8. Complete the sentences.

1. He was in a _____.

2. It's a hit-and-run. Get the _____ _____ _____.

3. The _____ _____ warned us early. It was a small fire.

4. But spray is _____. Keep it away from children.

5. You can buy a _____ _____ to keep in your house.

6. The sign says _____ _____, so you can not go in.

9

JOBS

JOBS 1

A. Is Tekaa here today?

B. No, she isn't. She has a part-time job.

A. Really?

B. Yes. She's

babysitting.
cleaning houses.
sewing shirts.
delivering newspapers.

• •

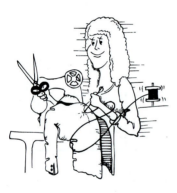

1._____   2._____

3. _____   4._____

1. Is he cooking?

Yes,_____.

2. Is he farming?

_____.

3. Is she sewing?

_____.

4. Is he working on a car?

_____.

5. Is he babysitting?

No, _____ _____.

He's _____ _____.

6. Is she delivering newspapers?

No, _____ _____.

She's_____ _____.

7. Is she babysitting?

No, _____ _____.

She's_____ _____.

8. Is she mowing lawns?

No, _____ _____.

She's_____ _____.

A. I can't come to the school anymore.

B. I'm sorry. Why not?

A. My husband got a full-time job. Nobody can take care of my baby.

B. What about your sister?

A. She wants to get a part-time job.

B. We'll miss you.

Ask your classmates.

Name	Do you have a job now?	What is your job?	Did you work before?	What was your job?
1.				
2.				
3.				

Job Search

Jobs are not easy to find. People find jobs in many ways. Here are four ideas to help you in your job search. 1). Some people get help finding a job from a friend or family member. Tell everyone you know that you are looking for a job. Maybe they can help you. 2). Some people find jobs in their neighborhood. Look for "help wanted" signs in restaurants and store windows. Then go in and ask about the job. 3). Some people read the classified ads in the newspaper. Then they call or go in for the application. 4). Some people had good jobs in their native countries. Here they have trouble with English. They may also need to update or learn more skills. Job training classes can help these people. Sometimes job training classes are free, but not always. Sometime there is a waiting list. Sometimes a job counselor will help the students get classes and then get jobs.

Circle true or false.

1.	It is difficult to find a job here.	true	false
2.	There are many ways to find a job here.	true	false
3.	"Help Wanted" means that there is a job there.	true	false
4.	Classified ads are in the newspaper.	true	false
5.	You can look in the newspaper for jobs.	true	false
6.	Job counselors can help you find a job.	true	false
7.	Finding a job is hard work.	true	false

A. My friend is looking for a part-time job.

B. There's a sign in the window at McJack's.

A. What should she do?

B. She should go inside and ask for an application.

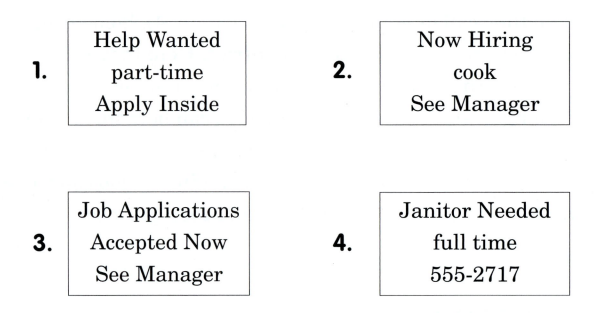

1.
Help Wanted
part-time
Apply Inside

2.
Now Hiring
cook
See Manager

3.
Job Applications
Accepted Now
See Manager

4.
Janitor Needed
full time
555-2717

1. What should you do for the janitor job?

_____

2. What should you do for the part time job?

_____

3. What is the full time job?

_____

4. What should you do for the cook job?

_____

> Wanted:
> Gardeners
> with exper.
> 555-0871

A. Hello.

B. Hello. I want to apply for the gardener job.

A. Do you have experience?

B. Yes, I do. I was a farmer for ten years.

A. You'll have to talk to the boss.
Call back tomorrow at 10 A.M.

B. O.K. Thank you.

JOB APPLICATION

Name: _____
　　　　　　　　Last name　　　　　　　　　　　　　First name

Address: _____
　　　　　　　　Number　　　　　　　　　　　　　Street

_____
　　　City　　　　　　　　　State　　　　　　　　Zip code

(_____) _____　　　_____
　　　　Telephone　　　　　　　Social Security Number

Are you over 18 years of age?　　yes ☐
　　　　　　　　　　　　　　　　　no ☐

Education:　Circle last grade completed:

Grade　5　6　7　8　　　High School　1　2　3　4　　　College　1　2　3　4

Name and address of last school attended: _____

_____

Do you have legal right to remain and work in the United States?　yes ☐
　　　　　　　　　　　　　　　　　　　　　　　　　　　　no ☐

Job experience?　yes ☐
　　　　　　　　　no ☐

What was your job? _____　How long? _____

Name and address of last job: _____

_____

Signature _____　Date _____

Cook Wanted
no exper. p/t
call for appt.
555-3284

A. Can I help you?

B. I want to ask about your ad for a cook.

A. Sure.

B. How much does it pay?

A. Starting pay is $5.50 an hour.

B. Are there benefits?

A. We have health insurance.

B. Could I have an application please?

A. Here it is.

B. Thank you.

· ·

Match

1. f/t _____   **a.** part-time, less than 40 hours

2. p/t _____   **b.** excellent

3. exper. _____   **c.** work

4. Xlnt. _____   **d.** hour

5. appt. _____   **e.** full-time, 40 hours

6. wk. _____   **f.** with experience

7. hr. _____   **g.** appointment

A.

```
Wanted
Babysitter
20 hr. wk.
No experience
555-0821
```

1. What is the job? _____

2. Do you need experience? _____

3. How many hours a week is it? _____

B.

```
Wanted:
Mechanic
2 yrs. exper. please
555-2141
Xlnt. job
```

4. What is the job? _____

5. Do you need experience?. _____

6. How much experience do you need?

_____

C.

```
Electronic
Assemblers
needed F/T
1yr. experience
```

7. What is the job? _____

8. Do you need experience? _____

9. Is it full-time or part-time? _____

D.

```
Wanted:
Housekeeper
No experience
555-3827
call for appt.
```

10. What is the job? _____

11. Do you need experience? _____

12. Do you need an appointment? _____

E.

```
Men and Women
wk. F/T or P/T
deliver
newspapers
No experience
```

13. What is the job? _____

14. Do you need experience? _____

15. Is it full-time or part-time? _____

Villa's Story

Villa is looking for a part-time job. She's a student now. She studies English in class everyday. She goes to the library and does homework every night. Villa is from Iran. In Iran, she was a nurse. She worked in a hospital. She took care of sick children in the hospital. Villa loved her job. She worked in the hospital for four years. She has four years experience as a nurse in Iran. She wants to work as a nurse again, but first she has to learn more English. Villa is studying English to be a nurse here.

Circle true or false.

1. Villa was a nurse in Iran.	true	false
2. She was a nurse for two years.	true	false
3. She worked in a doctor's office.	true	false
4. She didn't like her job.	true	false
5. Villa has job experience, but she needs more English.	true	false
6. Villa is studying English to be a nurse here.	true	false

Answer the questions.

7. Who is looking for a job?_____

8. What was her job in Iran? _____

9. How many years job experience does she have?

_____

10. What job does she want?

_____

Villa Mahmet wants to apply for a job. Her address is 1676 Fulton Street, Santa Ana, California. Her zip code is 92701. Her telephone number is 555-2000. Her date of birth is June 6, 1957. Her social security number is 007-32-8114.

Villa is from Iran. She went to school in her country. She went to elementary school, high school, and college. She was a nurse for two years. She has job experience. She has two years job experience as a nurse.

JOB APPLICATION

Name: _____
                        Last name   First name

Address: _____
                  Number   Street

_____
     City   State   Zip code

(   ) _____   _____
     Telephone   Social Security Number

Are you over 18 years of age?   yes ☐   no ☐

Education: Circle last grade completed:

Grade   5   6   7   8   High School   1   2   3   4   College   1   2   3   4

Name and address of last school attended: _____

_____

Do you have legal right to remain and work in the United States?   yes ☐   no ☐

Job experience?   yes ☐   no ☐

What was your job? _____ How long? _____

Name and address of last job: _____

_____

A. I have an appointment at the job training center.

B. What for?

A. I have to talk to my job counselor.

I want to enroll in

| electronic assembly. |
| machine shop. |
| auto repair. |
| power sewing. |
| _____. |

• •

1. Do you have a job training center in your area?

_____

2. What's the address of the job training center?

_____

3. Do you have a job counselor?

_____

4. What's your job counselor's name?

_____

5. What do you want to enroll in?

_____

A. I'm happy to tell you, you have the job.

B. Thanks. When do I start?

A. Be here tomorrow at 9:00 to fill out your insurance and tax forms. You can start next week.

B. I'll be here. Thanks

Remember to: **1.** Be on time **2.** Bring your social security card **3.** Shake hands **4.** Bring picture I.D.

What's the job?	What are the hours?	What's the salary?	What are the benefits?
1. Mechanic	7 am - 4 pm	$13 an hour	health
2. Assembler	2 pm - 11 pm	$9 an hour	health
3. Seamstress	1 pm - 5 pm	minimum wage	none

A. Pang got a job.

B. That's great! What days does she work?

A. Monday, Wednesday, and Saturday.

B. What are her hours?

A. From 4 P.M. to 9 P.M.

　　She works the night shift.

1. _____　　2. _____　　3. _____

Match

1. hired _____
2. laid-off _____
3. fired _____

4. quit _____
5. retired _____

a. You finished work after many years.
b. You will start a new job.
c. There was not enough work, so you stay home.
d. The boss said don't come back.
e. You stop working because you want to.

The Night Shift Schedule

	M	T	W	Th	F	Sat.	Sun.
Pang	4 - 9		4 - 9			4 - 9	
Lin		4 - 9		4 - 9			
Tom				5 - 9	5 - 9		5 - 9

1. What days does Lin work?

_____

2. What hours does Lin work?

_____

3. What days does Tom work?

_____

4. What hours does Tom work?

_____

5. What days does Pang work?

_____

6. What hours does Pang work?

_____

7. What shift do they work?

_____

A. I think there's a mistake on my paycheck.

B. What's wrong?

A. The amount isn't right.

B. Do you have the stub?

A. Yes, here it is. But I don't understand it.

B. Let's look at it.

- -

BIG CO.

FEB. 10, 1993

PAY TO ORDER OF ___KAO VUE___ $157.50

ONE HUNDRED FIFTY SEVEN $\frac{50}{100}$ DOLLARS

Mr. North

MR. NORTH, PRESIDENT

1. The part of the paycheck you keep is the _____.

2. The part of the paycheck you cash is the _____.

3. Who is the check made out to? _____

4. How much is the check for? _____

5. What is the company's name? _____

6. Who signed the check? _____

BIG CO.

FEB. 10, 1993

PAY TO ORDER OF __KAO VUE__ | $157.50 |

ONE HUNDRED FIFTY SEVEN $\frac{50}{100}$ DOLLARS

Mr. North

MR. NORTH, PRESIDENT

NAME: KAO VUE		
HOURS	GROSS PAY	NET PAY
35	$183.75	$157.50
F.I.C.A	FEDERAL TAX	STATE TAX
$5.25	$18.40	$2.60

Match

1. stub _____   a. total hours you work

2. hours _____   b. Social Security

3. gross pay _____   c. the money you take home

4. net pay _____   d. the money the state takes

5. F.I.C.A. _____   e. all the money you make

6. federal tax _____   f. the part of the paycheck you keep

7. state tax _____   g. the money the U.S. government takes.

NAME: KAO VUE		
HOURS	GROSS PAY	NET PAY
35	$ 183.75	$ 157.50
F.I.C.A	FEDERAL TAX	STATE TAX
$ 5.25	$ 18.40	$ 2.60

1. What is the name on the stub?

_____

2. What are the total hours worked?

_____

3. What is the net pay?

_____

4. What is the gross pay?

_____

5. How much does he pay to Social Security?

_____

6. How much does he pay to the state?

_____

7. How much does he pay to the U.S. government?

_____

A. What's this pink paper with my paycheck?

B. I'm sorry. You got laid off.

A. Why?

B. Because there isn't enough work for everyone.

A. When can I work again?

B. I'm not sure. I'll call you when there's more work.

· ·

Unemployment Information

If you lose your job, you may qualify for unemployment. Go to the unemployment office near you. Talk to a clerk in the unemployment office. Only the unemployment office can tell you about your job loss. Here are some things to remember about unemployment.

To qualify for unemployment:

1. You must have worked for a certain length of time.

2. You must have lost your job.

3. You must have worked at a job that paid into unemployment.

4. You must go to the unemployment office.

A. In my native country, I was a farmer.

B. What did you do each day?

A. I worked very hard. I grew corn, cucumbers, and rice.

B. Did you take care of animals too?

A. Yes, I did. I had some chickens and pigs. I never went to the grocery store.

B. Life was different there.

A. Yes. Life is very different here too.

Read the story.

Carlos the Baker

In his native country, Peru, Carlos was a baker. It was difficult work, but Carlos was happy. He worked six days a week, from four o'clock in the morning until six at night. He did a good job. His wife and their children worked there too. People bought their bread from Carlos every day. People liked to eat the cookies and bolillos from his bakery too.

Answer the questions.

1. Who was a baker? _____

2. Was his work easy or difficult? _____

_____

3. When did he work? _____

4. Did he like his job? Why or why not? _____

_____

Share your story with the class.

In my native country, _____ , I was a

_____ . It was _____ work. I worked

_____ days a week from _____ until_____ .

I did a_____ job.

Din's Story

Din had a job in an office building. He was a janitor there. He worked the night shift. He was in charge of many things at work. He was in charge of cleaning the offices, and he was in charge of small repairs. He did a good job, and he was never late to work. He was also friendly and everyone liked him. One night, his boss talked to all the janitors in the office building. The boss gave Din and another man a raise. Din was very excited. Then the boss gave Din the keys to the building. Now Din was in charge of locking up the office building too. He was very proud.

Circle true or false.

1. Din was a janitor in an office building. true   false

2. Din did a good job, but he was always
  late to work.   true   false

3. Three men got raises.   true   false

4. Din was in charge of many things.   true   false

5. Din was in charge of locking the
  office building.   true   false

6. Din was embarrassed and proud.   true   false

Change the false sentences to true sentences.

_____

_____

_____

Answer the questions.

1. Who was a janitor?

_____

2. Who gave Din a raise?

_____

3. What was Din's job?

_____

4. What was he in charge of doing?

_____

5. When did he work?

_____

6. Where did Din work?

_____

7. Why did Din get a raise?

_____

8. Why was Din proud?

_____

9. Was his job easy or difficult?

_____

10. Did he like his job? Why or why not?

_____

Answer the questions.

1. Are you working now?

_____

2. What is your job?

_____

3. Did you work in your country?

_____

4. What was your job?

_____

5. Was your job easy?

_____

6. Was your job difficult?

_____

7. Did you like your job?

_____

8. Do you want a job in the U.S.?

_____

9. What job do you want?

_____

10. How many years of experience do you have?

_____

Write the long answers to the above questions to make a story.

_____

_____

_____

_____

_____

_____

_____

_____

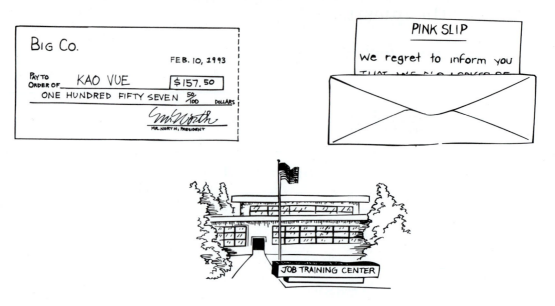

Review Unit 9. Complete the sentences.

1. My husband is studying auto repair at the _____. _____ _____.

2. When there isn't enough work for everyone, you get _____ _____.

3. She works at night. She works the _____ _____.

4. Jan works part-time. He helps put computers together. He's an _____.

5. Today is payday. I get my _____.

6. For many jobs you need _____ . It is not _____ to get a job in many places.